Your

Pension
Shortfall
Your
Retirement
Rescue Plan

Gill Alton

Copyright

Contents

Section One

Your Pension Shortfall – How Big? and Why?

Section Two

The Advantages and Strengths of Property Investment

Section Three

Property Investment as a Pension – the Proof

Section Four

Your Step–by–Step Retirement Rescue Plan

A logical and detailed programme for you to follow step by step, to reach a happy and financially sound Retirement

Acknowledgements

Writing this book has been very much a personal crusade and I admit when started I had absolutely no appreciation of the time, effort and dedication involved.

Without the following people however, the story in this book would never have been told.

Firstly, to my husband, **Richard Alton** – thanks for keeping everything ship shape and running smoothly while I've focussed on this book.

To my two wonderful children, **Annalise and Andersen** – your support of Mum has been unquestionable, even when you've heard the all too familiar cry, 'I'm off to work on my book'. I hope when you see this book published you will realise you too can, with sufficient effort, achieve anything you put your mind to.

To my Mind Coach, **Alan Whitton** of West Essex Hypnotherapy – The work we have done together has kept me focussed and determined to succeed. In moments of creative struggle your skills in helping me move past the mental blocks has been pure brilliance. Thanks.

To my friend **Kim Worthington** – thank you so much for coming to my aid at such short notice. So very kind of you.

To **Stephanie Hale** of Oxford Writers – Your support in getting this book into print has removed much stress from me, what a relief. Thank you.

And finally to my parents, **Maureen and Brian Spratling** (and particularly my Mum) – the biggest thanks has to be reserved for you. From the moment I told you on the phone 'Mum I'm going to write a book' you have been nothing but supportive. From me monopolising your retired Accountancy skills to help develop and check over 300+ pages of spreadsheet, to you proof reading version after version of this book, your input has been priceless. I couldn't have done it without you. Huge thanks from one very appreciative daughter.

Introduction

When I was young and worked in the corporate world, I believed that 'retiring' meant being given the Golden Key to an exclusive club. Joining the club was something to get excited about, and colleagues would count down the days till they earned their *'pass'*.

When the day arrived it involved parties and being showered with cards and balloons all saying:

'Happy Retirement'

And

'after years of hard–work and dedication it's time to take a permanent vacation'

Retirement was something to celebrate!

Those of us still working knew when our time came we too would be able to join this elite group where the years are filled with endless golf, panama hats, pruning roses in a cottage garden, happy smiling faces and walking hand in hand with the one we love along a tropical beach of white sand with crystal clear blue sea lapping at our feet. Retirement represented the time in our lives when we would be financially worry–free, and able to enjoy many activities because time would be on our side.

Unfortunately, however, the story has changed, although the marketing literature has not!

Now those of us left working are being sold a dream which is totally unachievable for millions and millions. Your right to a 'carefree, dream like' retirement doing the things you want to, rather than have to, is no more real today than the mythical characters who bring magic and fun into our children's lives.

The problem is, growing up to realise the Tooth Fairy is make–believe simply takes away some of the innocence of childhood but finding out the retirement you dreamt of, and have saved hard for over many years, is fictitious can be life changing.

To help illustrate the harsh reality of how much the storyboard has changed, please let me share with you my own experience. This, and the stories from many clients we have met through our Mortgage Business who have faced the horror of a pension shortfall with little or no time left to change their future, has spurred me on to write this book. I hope it will empower others to change the future they are heading towards before it is too late.

How to achieve a 90% drop in your Pension!

Twenty three years ago, when I graduated and secured my first employed position with an American corporation, I joined a Final Salary Pension Scheme. My salary reflected my position as a newly qualified graduate and I remained in the scheme for just four years before moving to another organization. I froze my pension with the employer when I left.

A couple of years later, aged 26, I was approached by my Bank who offered me a Pensions Review. At that stage retirement was something that happened to 'old people with greying hair', and my projected retirement date was further in the future than the years since my birth. Four years of pension contributions seemed minimal and inconsequential and I had absolutely no understanding of the power of the Final Salary Pension Scheme I had in my hands.

The bank provided growth projections on their Personal Pension which showed how they only needed to achieve an annual growth rate of 10.51% pa to out–perform my frozen pension scheme. A performance level they confirmed in writing was definitely achievable. In my naivety I transferred a 'Guaranteed Pension' to a pension scheme which offered no such promises.

Approximately six years ago I woke up to the stupidity of my actions, however my complaint was rejected and I was forced to write–off my losses as an expensive learning curve.

February this year, however, I was tracked down by the Bank who admitted that they had indeed misled me.

If I had left my pension frozen with my previous employer, because of the guaranteed elements within the scheme, it is projected that it would have generated an inflation linked retirement income of approximately £3,000 per annum. Moving my fund to a scheme where there is no guarantee of outcome and I am personally exposed (just like a Defined Contribution Scheme) to the performance of the Stock Market, Fund Charges and Annuity Rates, my pension fund is currently projected to deliver an income of approximately £300 pa.

A reduction of 90%!

I am one of the lucky ones as the Bank has now admitted misleading me, so I wait to be compensated. The compensation I receive will go towards reducing my investment mortgage debt, so I can utilise it to gain more security and control, by building my pension provision from property.

However, for millions the reality of their pension exposure with the mass movement in recent years to Defined Contribution Pension Schemes, has not yet been understood. And, when grasped, the horror and shock of the reality will leave many people who have acted sensibly and saved hard, reeling.

My passion behind writing this book has been to help demonstrate the 'Golden dream of a retirement filled with fun and no money worries' funded by a Defined Contribution Pension Scheme, is a reality which has unfortunately gone up in smoke. Only by increasing your understanding are you able to make informed decisions which will allow you to step out from the masses and take action. Action – before time runs out.

This book shares the cold hard facts of the effect of the current economic reality on our retirement dreams, before sharing a realistic and achievable Rescue Plan, which is designed to let you rebuild the vision of the retirement you deserve.

This book is not about a 'get rich quick scheme', those that know me know that's not my style; it's about following a controlled and purposeful pathway to change your future.

If this book changes just a handful of people's retirement for the better, then it will have been worthwhile writing.

1. Why you Need to Read this Book

What makes this book different from any of the other pension or property books?

Answer

Because this book has been written to take you on a journey. A journey which will scare you, educate you and then provide you with a solution.

In particular, this book has been written because, in the UK, we are heading towards a huge Pension Crisis. A Pension Crisis which, although mentioned in the Press, is I believe misunderstood and ignored by the vast majority. Perhaps because, unsettling though it may be, these articles only illustrate the base of the pension mountain that we have to climb. The sheer size and steepness is hard to portray and often underestimated.

But take time to understand how dramatically the world has changed, and it will become clear that the Pension Rule book has been challenged in every respect. Placing your faith solely on a crumbling pathway which relies on the same old traditional savings route for retirement is a sure–fire way of ensuring that you are teetering on the very edge of existence in your later years. Barely clinging on, at a time when you should be enjoying life.

We are entering uncharted Pension territory!

This book has, therefore, been written to help you understand the severity of the challenge we are facing both as a country and individuals. It's deliberately packed full of facts and figures so you understand the shocking truth of exactly how severely your pathway to the happy retirement you were promised has been eroded.

I want you to feel uncomfortable, because only by feeling uncomfortable will you take the actions to strengthen your route, while you have time on your side.

Having explained 'Why' you need to sit up and take action, this book will then go on to explain in detail 'How' your ultimate Pension Strategy will counterbalance all the negative elements impacting your pension savings. You will be provided with evidence to help you recognize how the right type of Property Investment can indeed meet your requirements and reinforce your retirement by establishing a durable and reliable pathway.

A retirement pathway which will allow you to traverse the pension mountain, while others are left struggling.

Finally, this book will explain clearly "How" to establish and implement your own enduring "Retirement Rescue Plan".

This Pension Crisis will not go away; how it impacts you will be determined by the actions you take today.

You need to be one step ahead and take responsibility for your retirement years and you need to start now, particularly if time is not on your side.

So you must read this book if:

- You already save into a pension, but your Retirement Plans are based on a Defined Contribution (Money Purchase) Scheme.

- You are a homeowner and you have watched as your savings in the bank have earned a pittance over the last few years.

- You've already realized your retirement plans are under threat, but you are struggling to step forward and commit to a plan which can rescue you.

- You are established in life, but are worried by the limited time you have to address any pension shortfall.

- Or alternatively, you are currently sitting on the sidelines wondering what 'all the retirement fuss' is about and have started to worry that you may have missed something important!

- Finally, you have a property education or a Hands–Free investment business and you want to help educate potential clients with facts and figures, to show how they can follow a Plan to solve their Pension Shortfall.

This book will clarify the confusing maelstrom of our Economy and your Retirement Planning, so that you can understand why **'Your Pension Shortfall'** has occurred, and how you can implement **'Your Retirement Rescue Plan'**.

Disclaimer

Before we progress I do however need to share the following Disclaimer.

Although I have created and analysed more than 300 spreadsheet pages to write this book, I am not a qualified Investment Advisor. Therefore, I am not qualified to provide personal investment advice. As such all information found within this book, including any ideas, opinions, views, predictions, forecasts, commentaries or suggestions expressed or implied herein, are for informational, or educational purposes only and should not be construed as personal investment advice. While the information provided is believed to be accurate, it may include errors or inaccuracies.

I will not and cannot be held liable for any actions you take as a result of anything you read here.

In addition 'David', is based on a fictitious individual and therefore any resemblance to any real persons, living or dead, is purely coincidental. I could just as easily have selected 'Lisa', or 'Susan', as the story in this book applies to either gender.

Now that's over, let's begin!

2. How to Read this Book

To help you navigate your way through, this book is written in four sections:

Section One:

Starts by providing you with a shocking realistic example, to demonstrate the potential size of your Pension Shortfall, before going on to explain the factors which have combined to create this lethal retirement scenario.

Section Two:

Concentrates on introducing the solution to your Pension Shortfall. It specifically explains how the proposed solution will deal with each of the situations that negatively influence your current Pension performance as identified in Section One.

Section Three:

Focuses on your Rescue Plan and shares with you the results of the comprehensive financial modelling completed within the book. The focus is on proving, with facts and figures, how property investment can provide a retirement income to sit alongside your existing pension provision. So filling your pension income gap and strengthening your financial situation.

Every attempt has been made to answer upfront your *'what if'* questions so that you fully understand and are completely comfortable with the Rescue Plan and the action you need to take.

Section Four:

Provides you with your Step by Step Retirement Rescue Plan. This will allow you to implement your own personalised plan to achieve the retirement of your dreams.

Ideally I would recommend you navigate your way through the book reading each Section sequentially, as this strengthens your understanding of why you cannot afford to do nothing.

(To me 'Status Quo' is simply the name of a Rock Band, it doesn't represent a sound financial investment strategy on which to base your retirement).

However, if you are the type of person who likes to get directly to the answer you can jump straight in at Section Three, before progressing to Section Four.

My only caveat to this approach is – if you don't understand a subject being discussed, go back and take time to seek its origin in the first two Sections.

I hope you enjoy the read and the messages contained within the book compel you to take action.

Section One

Your Pension Shortfall –
How big? and Why?

3. Are You David?

Let's meet David!

David is about to enjoy his 50th Birthday. He is an IT Project Manager and in his younger years he changed jobs several times, but he settled at 35 years old and has been with his current employer since then. His starting salary at 35 was £27,343 but with inflationary rises (note 1, page 22) his salary has now risen to £42,780pa (note 2, page 22).

David enjoys his job and has no desire to embrace any further Managerial career changes, so he anticipates that he will be awarded with inflationary rises each year until he retires.

David is a responsible type of person, so when he joined his current employer he decided it was time to start investing for his retirement, even though it seemed years off at the time. So, since the age of 35 he has been contributing 4% of his salary to the Company Pension Scheme, and his employer has been contributing 5%. Under his Company's Pension Scheme the 'Total Expense Ratio' (note 3) quoted for his pension fund is 1.5% pa.

David is a Basic Rate Tax Payer (note 4) so over the last 15 years David has benefited from 20% tax relief on his pension contributions.

He is married with two children. His wife has been the 'home maker' and she only rejoined the workforce when the children were teenagers in their final years at secondary school. Since then she has held a variety of part time administrative roles and is currently working within a school.

David's wife hasn't contributed to a Personal Pension and on their projections she will have 15 – 20 years of qualifying National Insurance Contributions by the time she reaches retirement. Since she will need 35 years for a full State Pension, they have always considered any retirement income she does receive as a bonus, and together their focus has been on ensuring David's pension is sufficient to provide for them both.

David has just received his Annual Pension Statement and the value of his fund currently stands at £58,725. (note 5)

He notices when he looks at this Pension Statement that his projected retirement income is based on his fund continuing to grow at either 2%, 5% or 8% per annum (note 6), which is lower than previous projections. Based on the 5% compound growth rate, if David continues to contribute to his Pension on the current basis of 4% of his salary (with an additional 5% by the Employer and Tax Relief) then his pension pot will be worth £203,120 at retirement.

David has read in the Press that annuity rates have fallen but has not actually looked at what this means for him personally. However, having now seen that the projected future value of his pension has also fallen, he is a little nervous and armed with his latest Annual Pension Statement, feels it would be a good time to sit down and work out how his retirement plans are tracking.

David is only looking to insure a single life in retirement, because the plan is that his wife will sell the house and downsize should he pre–decease her. He does however want his pension income to increase by a fixed 3% per annum, as his parents chose a level pension and he has witnessed their increasing struggle to make ends meet. He also wants his pension to pay out for an agreed term, say five years, so should he die early into his retirement at least his estate will receive a minimum amount from his pension fund, and it won't all simply be lost.

Knowing his requirements, David turns to the internet to find the best rate for a 'Single life, 3% escalation, 5yr guarantee', and discovers it is 4.073%. (note 7)

Based on a projected pension pot of £203,120 David calculates his retirement income will be:

£203,120 x 4.073% = **£8,273 p.a.**

David is speechless at how low this is, because he has always considered himself to be diligent and forward thinking in starting to plan for his retirement 30 years before he wished to retire. He had already calculated that on today's prices he needed a pre–tax retirement income of £24,500 (Please refer to the Appendix (page 239) for a breakdown of David's expenses and note 8), which he didn't feel was greedy, so allowing for State Pension at £144 per week his personal pension will need to deliver £17,012 at today's prices. By the time he comes to retire in 16 years this would need to increase to £26,273 (note 9) to maintain its purchasing power.

David has an annual pension shortfall of:

£26,273 – £8,273 = **£18,000**

The reality has hit David hard. He feels tremendously worried and isolated, and fears he doesn't have the time or money needed to rectify this pension shortfall. Not knowing what to do, David is completely overwhelmed.

The graphic below illustrates the size of David's Pension Shortfall and at the end of this Chapter you will find a detailed summary of David's Pension as it currently stands.

Figure 1

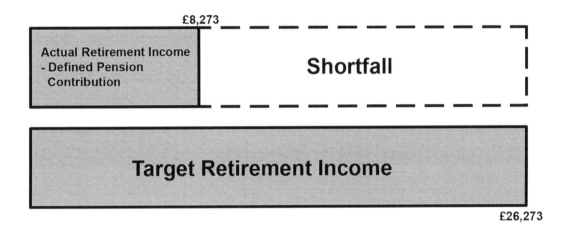

David's Pension Shortfall

£8,273

| Actual Retirement Income - Defined Pension Contribution | Shortfall |

Target Retirement Income

£26,273

Are you David? If you are, don't panic – keep reading!

For simplicity I have concentrated on one character throughout this book, David. As we know David is employed and contributing to a Company Pension, however the same principles apply within this book whether self–employed or part–time and contributing to a personal pension.

In each scenario your pension shortfall will vary dependent on your personal pension circumstances and the income you require in your retirement.

Notes

Note 1: Inflation has been calculated at 2.94% pa. This is the average inflation over the last 15 years (December 1997 – December 2012) Source ONS

Note 2: Median Salary Project Manager IT £42,712. As at 17th April 2013. Payscale.com

Note 3: Total Expense Ratio – this is the total cost of all the charges incurred by a Pension Fund and includes: Annual Management Charge, Administrative Fees, Regulatory Fees, Marketing Fees, Directors' Fees, Audit Fees, Legal and Other Fees

Note 4: In tax year 2012/2013 the Basic Rate Tax of 20% was payable on earnings between £8,105 – £42,475. In the tax year 2013/ 2014 it has been moved to £9,440 – £41,450. So David has now just dipped into the Higher Rate Tax band. To keep it simple within this illustration however we will be working with David as a Basic Rate Tax Payer. This means over the last 15 years David has benefited from 20% tax relief on his pension contributions.

Note 5: David's starting contribution at 35 years old was £91 per month, the fund has grown by 5% per annum and Fund fees of 1.5% are deducted at the end of each year. He has made payments for 15 years.

Note 6: The new FCA Pension Projection Guidelines due to go live in April 2014

Note 7: Rates valid as at 18th April 2013 from Hargreaves Lansdown site
http://www.hl.co.uk/pensions/annuities/annuity–best–buy–rates

Note 8: According to the Scottish Widows Pension Report 2012 the average 70 year old would feel comfortable with this level of household income.

Figure 2

David's Pension Summary	

Assumptions	
Average inflation throughout working life is	2.94%
David's salary has risen in line with inflation	
David's Pension contributions have been	4%
Davids' Employer's contributions have been	5%
David's pension fund annual interest earned	5%
Fund Management Fees (TER) pa	1.50%
Annuity Rate for Single Life, 3% escalation 5 Yr guarantee	4.073%

David is now 50	
His current salary is	£42,780
His current pension fund is valued at	£58,725
David's desired retirement income at today's prices	£24,500
The current State Pension at £144 per week is	£7,488
Therefore, income to be generated by pension is	£17,012

When David is Age 65	
His salary will be	£66,070
His pension fund will be worth	£203,120
This will buy an annuity of	£8,273
With inflation, income to be generated by pension will be	£26,273

David's Retirement Income at Age 65	
Retirement Income to be generated by pension	£26,273
Less Annuity Income	£8,273
David's Pension Shortfall	**£18,000**

4. How the World has Changed

Before we start to discuss why property can provide a valuable addition to your pension it would be good to understand the history of pensions; how things have changed and the impact this will have.

We often hear or read about the 'downfall' of pensions but without some background knowledge and an understanding of how all the elements fit together it is difficult to appreciate the severity of the problem. It's like simply seeing the tip of the iceberg, but failing to appreciate the extensive damage occurring below the water. This book is designed to share with you some hard hitting facts to help you understand the full picture, so you can make informed and timely decisions, allowing you to circumvent the crisis coming our way. This Chapter will provide an overview of how our existing Retirement Plans have been challenged on every side.

What's happened to your Pension?

The State Pension 1909

Firstly, let's start by understanding the pressure the State Pension is under.

The State Pension was 100 years old in 2009 having been introduced by Lloyd George. From 1st January 1909 the pension offered five shillings a week (seven shillings and sixpence for a married couple) to all retired workers over 70 years old. The level was deliberately set low to encourage people to make their own additional provision and there were some fairly tight criteria controlling eligibility.

For example, claimants needed to earn less than £31.50 per year and be of 'good character'. Those who were already in receipt of Poor Relief; in a lunatic asylum; in prison (and even for a decade after their release); convicted of drunkenness or guilty of 'habitual failure to work' were excluded. Unlike today!

When the State Pension was first paid over 100 years ago, the UK population was 38 million and relatively few people lived past 70 years; so the numbers entitled to benefit were limited. In fact, the life expectancy of a boy born in 1901 was only 45 years old and a girl 49 years old, so not only was reaching the grand age of 70 years a significant achievement but the likelihood of requiring pension income for many years was very low.

Today however, there are 12.4million (2012) pensioners (an increase of 5.6m in the last 60 years) and this expansion is predicted to continue with 14million pensioners by 2020. The current basic State Pension being amended in 2016 is only £5,587 pa and although this can be enhanced by Pension Credits, Council Tax Benefit and Housing Benefit, these additional elements are means tested.

Even allowing for all these enhancements, the money you would receive could be well below that which the Joseph Rowntree Foundation considers to be the Poverty Line for a single pensioner in the UK – £8,254 per annum. In fact on this basis it is predicted that one in five will retire in 2013 below the Poverty Line. A shocking statistic! (Source: The Guardian, 22nd May 2013 – 'One in Five retiring in 2013 will be below poverty line')

As we know from the media, the cost of funding the State Pension is growing as the number of the elderly continues to rise. The media sensationalize the need for us to work beyond 65 but we are living longer and it's only taking the pension eligibility date back to its original starting point of 70 years of age.

The pressure on the State is compounded because it also has the responsibility of providing occupational pensions for the public sector and in 2009 this cost was estimated at £650billion (Government calculations) and £1trillion by the CBI and other bodies. So not insignificant!

Life Expectancy and the UK Population

The pressure on the public purse strings is greater than ever and one of the major contributory factors has already been alluded to – the significant increase in the UK population and in particular our ageing population. In fact, since 1952 the percentage of pensioners in the population has increased by 6%, taking the total to 20%.

The chart over the page produced from data from the Office for National Statistics, illustrates how the population of England and Wales has grown since 1801. The 1911 Census recorded 36 million residents. By 2011 that had risen to 56 million, an increase of 56%, and already we are being advised that the population is heading towards 70 million by 2027.

Figure 3

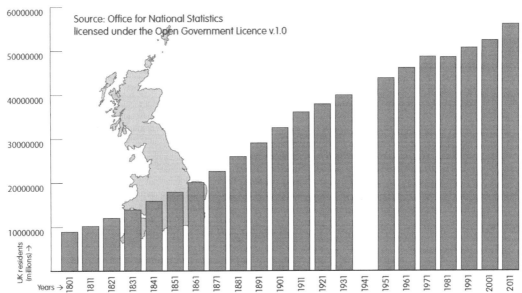

Residents 1801 – 2011 England and Wales

Source: Office for National Statistics
licensed under the Open Government Licence v.1.0

Early censuses recorded population present, rather than usual residents. There was no census in 1941, due to the Second World War. Comparison with 2001 and 1991 is based on mid-year population estimates for those years, Comparison for 1981 and earlier is based on census results.

So not only has the size of our population grown, but the demographics have also changed, with our population ageing significantly. The quote below is taken directly from the Office of National Statistics Website and their report – Summary UK Population Projected to Reach 70 million by Mid.2027. Released 26th October 2011.

The UK population is projected to increase by 4.9 million to 67.2 million over the ten year period to 2020. This increase is equivalent to an average annual rate of growth of 0.8 per cent.

If past trends continue, the population will continue to grow, reaching 73.2 million by 2035. This is due to natural increase (more births than deaths) and because it is assumed there will be more immigrants than emigrants (a net inward flow of migrants).

In common with other European countries, the UK has an ageing population. The population is projected to continue ageing with the average (median) age rising from 39.7 years in 2010 to 39.9 years in 2020 and 42.2 years by 2035.

As a result, despite the forthcoming increases to state pension age under current legislation, the number of people of state pension age (SPA) is projected to increase by 28 per cent from 12.2 million to 15.6 million by 2035. This reflects the higher number of people born immediately after the 2nd World War and also those who were born in the 1960s 'baby boom' reaching state pension age within the 25 year period to 2035'.

The graph over the page helps illustrate the massive expansion of pensioners in the next 20 years. The dark bars show the size of the UK population in relation to age in 2010, the light bars show the projected size of the population, in relation to age by 2035. In particular, you can see the big difference between the two shaded bars once the age of 60 years old is reached. This difference highlights the extent of the size of our 'ageing population' problem.

So if the Government has a problem now supporting us all, imagine what it will be like in the future.

The influx of immigrants to the UK and the increase in our life expectancy are all creating pressure points on an already overstretched social pot. As previously stated, the life expectancy for a boy born in 1901 was only 45 years and for a girl 49 years. It is little wonder Lloyd George felt secure in setting the pension age at 70 years. Now, however, the life expectancy of a child born in 2010 in the UK is 78 years for boys and 82 years for girls. An increase of 73% and 67% respectively.

Figure 4

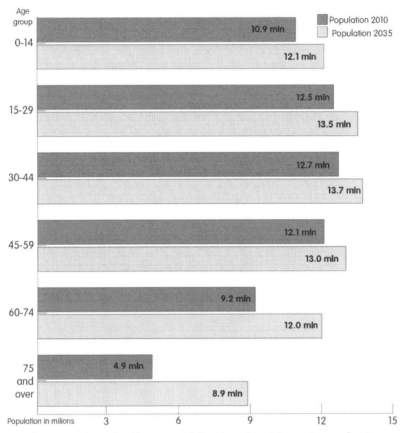

The changing shape of the UK.
Age structure of the UK population

Age group

Population 2010
Population 2035

0-14: 10.9 mln / 12.1 mln

15-29: 12.5 mln / 13.5 mln

30-44: 12.7 mln / 13.7 mln

45-59: 12.1 mln / 13.0 mln

60-74: 9.2 mln / 12.0 mln

75 and over: 4.9 mln / 8.9 mln

Population in millions — 3, 6, 9, 12, 15

* Working age and pensionable age populations based on state pension age for given year. Between 2010 and 2020, state pension age will change from 65 years for men and 60 years for women, to 65 years for both sexes. Between 2024 and 2046, state pension age will increase in three stages from 65 years to 68 years for both sexes.

Source: Adapted from data from the Office for National Statistics Licensed under the Open Government Licence v 1.0

Based on these facts it's hardly surprising the Government is tightening the purse strings – particularly when you add into the equation the financial crisis and recent recession. As the number of unemployed hovers around 2.49million (July 2013), those working and contributing to the State Pension, through their National Insurance payments, have an increasingly unrealistic task to provide sufficient funds.

In fact, in its current form the State Pension is nothing more than a Ponzi Scheme, whereby those joining (in this case the UK workforce) prop up the scheme for those wanting to draw their pensions. Unfortunately, such a scheme only works if new people are constantly joining the bottom and the revenue they contribute exceeds the amount paid out. As we can see from the illustrations this situation is becoming unbalanced – a house of cards that could easily collapse.

It's now naïve to think that the revenue contributed during their working years, by those now reaching retirement, will be sufficient to support them. Unfortunately it has long since been spent!

Pensions

Thankfully, not everyone is relying on the State Pension to support them. They have made other pension provision. So now let's turn our attention to understand this in more detail.

There are two kinds of pension:

- Defined Benefit (often known as a Final Salary Scheme)
- Defined Contribution (often known as Money Purchase Scheme)

Defined Benefit (Final Salary)

These schemes represent the Rolls Royce of pensions. They are offered by employers, Local Councils and Government, with both the employer and the employee making a contribution. However, the pension received is not determined by how much money is paid in, nor how the investment has performed, but rather by the final salary of the employee. This type of pension is particularly powerful if you join the company at a lower level and work your way up via promotion, as your pension is based on your tenure and salary at retirement. This income is then guaranteed.

However, with the change in the UK demographics, the Defined Benefit scheme has also come under pressure in recent years due to the 'guaranteed' nature of the payout. Companies and the Government have found that they are responsible for an ever increasing number of pensioners with longer life expectancy, yet have a diminishing active workforce (due perhaps to improvements in technology and systemization), and the numbers no longer stack up. This has led to many employers closing their Defined Benefit scheme to new entrants. Many have now gone one step further and frozen their schemes at a date in time, moving all employees to a Defined Contribution or Money Purchase scheme.

Defined Contribution (Money Purchase)

The title gives this one away – the money put into the scheme is 'defined' – that is an agreed percentage from your salary and from your employer. The unknown element is how much you will receive as a pension at the end of the process. This is because there are two important factors that influence the result.

- The monetary value of your pension pot when you reach retirement age.

- The annuity rates at the time you buy your annuity and convert your saved pot into an annual pension.

Because there are no guarantees you can understand why employers are transferring their employees to a Defined Contribution scheme, as the risk moves from the employer to the employee, limiting the employer's exposure to Stock Market fluctuations, banking crises, etc.

Auto Enrolment

Auto Enrolment introduced by the Government in October 2012 represents a massive shake up of the pension industry. The Government's aim is to increase the number of people actually saving into a pension plan (over and above the State Pension) but the contribution levels are extremely small, starting at 1%, then rising in later years.

So, although it is a good first step, it does not solve the problem of potential poverty in retirement, particularly as it is a Defined Contribution scheme so the risk still remains with the individual. It will, however, force all employers to support their employees from age 22 to retirement, by making monthly contributions on their behalf.

Personal Pension

A personal pension scheme (also known as a Private Pension) is a type of Defined Contribution Pension scheme in which an individual contributes part of their salary to a financial institution, however there is no additional contribution by an employer. Their contributions however do still attract tax relief.

SIPPS (SELF Invested Personal Pension)

A SIPP is a Self Invested Personal Pension, as the name implies the money saved is again based on the personal contribution, as there is no additional input from an employer.

SIPP charges are much higher than those imposed on Company schemes as they are far more complex, offering as many as eighteen different asset classes in which to invest, although not all providers offer the complete range.

Few people choose to invest in SIPPs because, as their name suggests, they are 'Self Invested'. This means you have far greater control over where your money is invested but with control comes responsibility. As most people have little or no knowledge of investing, and the different markets available, it is easy to understand why the majority prefer to leave the investing to a Fund Manager of a Mutual Fund.

5. Saving for your Retirement

Shockingly, given the current state of the economy and the State Pension, the number of people who are actually making their own pension provision is worryingly low.

Auto Enrolment is a sticking plaster to mend a break – but at least it is a sticking plaster and as the contributions increase over time may even morph into a bandage. But it will struggle to do little else, particularly as there is considerable negative press coverage concerning the charges being incurred by the schemes.

When saving into a pension scheme there is nothing truer than 'starting early and benefiting from compounding interest'. However, this is not the format that most people follow and recent figures from the Office of National Statistics (ONS Sept 2011) show that only 2.9million of the 29 million employed in the Private Sector are contributing to a Company Pension Scheme. This equates to the lowest number ever recorded since the ONS began compiling the data in 1953.

Of the remainder, 6 million workers are in the Public Sector and a rather impressive 5.3million (88 %) of these save into a workplace pension scheme. Perhaps this higher percentage is because to date the Public Sector has been less impacted by the move from Defined Benefit to Defined Contribution.

However, Public Sector employees are in for a change. Change in the amount they need to contribute, the number of years they are required to contribute and how the basis of their Pensions are now calculated. i.e rather than take their Final Salary, calculations are now based on 'career average earnings'. This move alone is projected by the Pensions Policy Institute to see average pension income fall from 23% of their salary to just 15%.

The strikes in 2012 were a direct consequence of Public Sector employees not wishing to embrace these changes and there are further strikes threatened. Unfortunately, the Pension Crisis is a real issue being faced by millions, both in the Private and Public Sectors and as an economy we are very much sitting on the edge of a massive precipice.

The severity is apparent when you add those paying into company schemes to the 6.4 million Self Employed individuals paying into a Personal Pension and you realise out of a total workforce of 29 million, only 14.6 million are making any provision for their future (2.9m Private, 5.3m Public and 6.4m Self Employed). On this basis a massive

14.4m are making no provision at all, or at least they weren't until Auto Enrolment kicked in.

For many this will be 'too little too late', as the average retirement income expected has risen to £24,500, almost double that which the average saver retiring at 65 is set to receive – £13,000.

In reality there is a huge pension savings shortfall in the UK and research from the Department for Works and Pensions (published Sept 2013) has found that workers on middle and high incomes are likely to face a sharp drop in income when they retire. In–fact, almost 400,000 of today's higher–earning workers – on more than £35,400 a year– will end up among the poorest 20% of pensioners. A frightening statistic, which supports the analysis we have completed for David.

Steve Webb – Pensions Minster told the Daily Telegraph (13 September 2013)

'People want the same sort of standard of living when they retire as when they were working, but unless you are putting a significant amount by, you could face a significant drop in your standard of living'

'It's tempting to think that not saving enough is just a problem for people on modest incomes, but it goes all the way up the income ladder'

'We found some of the people who will have spent their working lives at the top of the scale could spend their retirements at the bottom if they don't do something about it'.

6. Pension Schemes and Charges

So far we have learnt about:

1. The pressure the State Pension is under due to
    i.   The population growth
    ii.   The ageing population

2. The changes in pension schemes

3. The low numbers of people actually investing for their retirement.

But we have not covered the performance of the actual money which is being invested in Pension Schemes.

Pension Schemes are run by Fund Managers and, through their careful, selective and knowledgeable investment strategies, it is the Fund Manager's role to grow your pension pot.

Within a Company Pension Scheme you have little or no control over where your money is actually invested. And with the recent bankruptcy/merging of many companies due to the financial crisis and subsequent global recession, the shares of some companies have become worthless. As a result millions have simply been wiped off the value of pension funds.

For example, Northern Rock shares fell from a high of 1,251p in February 2007 to an all–time low of 90p just prior to nationalization, with shareholders losing everything at this stage. Then in 2009 the collapse of RBS saw their shares lose almost 70%. Add into the mix 'Act of God' events such as the explosion on BP's Deepwater Horizon Offshore Oil Rig, which caused BP's shares to crash over two months from £655.40 to a record low of £298, (wiping off £55bn off the Company's market value) and you can see how shareholders are left exposed.

Since Pension Funds are one of the major shareholders in large companies, the knock–on effect on Pension Funds is often forgotten, but highly significant. For example, most British Pensions focus on the FTSE100 companies and certainly with regard to BP most Funds invested around 8% of their UK Equity holdings in BP, (i.e. around 1% of their overall fund) so that crash had a big impact on Fund values.

Outperforming the Stock Market is a huge challenge for the Fund Manager and takes great skill, and to my mind a great big helping of 'luck'.

One thing is for sure, however, as a member of a Company Pension Scheme the security of your future is very much out of your hands. Once your contribution is made the next time you are aware of its performance, is when you receive your Annual Pension Statement.

And unlike Endowment Policies, there is no coloured warning light system, so you need to take time to review the forecasts and understand the projections and what they mean to you.

Pension Charges – Total Expense Ratio

You're not alone if you have left a Company Fund Manager to have control of your future.

However, Fund Managers charge for their services and these services have received considerable press coverage in recent months, spurred on by the underlying poor performance of the Funds themselves.

The introduction of the Financial Services Retail Distribution Review has been aimed at making Independent Financial Advisor Fees far more transparent, but I believe there is still some way to go before individuals effectively understand how charges and fees affect Pension Fund performance over the long term. For example, we tend to focus on the 'Annual Management Charge', but forget to consider all the other additional charges associated with a Pension Fund, all of which eat into the end fund value.

The 'Total Expense Ratio' (TER) is a more accurate reflection of true fund costs, and includes the following additional costs on top of the Annual Management Charge:

- Administration Fees
- Regulatory Fees
- Marketing Fees
- Director's Fees
- Audit Fees
- Legal Fees
- Other Fees

The diagram below from www.monevator.com shows how, just like an iceberg, the real danger is in that which is below the water level, concentrating on that which you can see above the water is highly misleading.

Figure 5

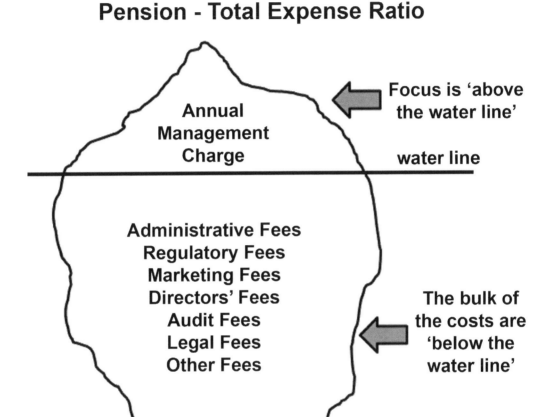

Low percentages of 1% or 2% never sound that significant but they can have an enormous impact in the long term. For example, add another 2% for Administrative costs such as the cost of stamp duty on share purchases, or stock broking fees associated with share and bond trading and you can easily take your TER to 3% – 4% per year.

Over the lifetime of the pension that extra 2% can result in a halving of the pension benefit. It really is an example of the power of compounding working against you!

So how has the Stock Market performed over the past 10/15 years?

Now we understand more about Pension Funds and how they charge us, how has the Stock Market performed in recent years? After–all this is where the Pension Funds are vested.

Without doubt, the market has experienced some huge challenges, which have impacted its performance. The Stock Market's performance is basically a measure of investors' confidence and as we know market confidence has been extremely low over recent years.

In fact at the end of the nineties the FTSE 100 was 22% below its position at the beginning of the decade, and between 2000 and 2010 the FTSE 100 returned a little less than 7%, so you can understand how Fund Managers have had their work cut out, continually trying to buck the market and win high.

This underperformance is reflected in the results of most Pension Funds. As a result, the Financial Conduct Authority (previously known as the FSA) ruled that as of April 2014 all pension providers are required to update their "pension calculators" to provide a more accurate reflection of reality i.e. 2%, 5% and 8%. Currently, most illustrations provided are calculated on the basis of compound growth rates of either 5%, 7% or 9% per annum, with most website projections focused on the mid–point of 7% (you need to go into an additional screen to change the projection to 5% or 9%). This may not sound a massive difference, but when the power of compounding is taken into account, it is anticipated that this change alone will act as a wake–up call to 16 million people.

This 'update on reality' is desperately needed as it will help avoid the situation of people reaching retirement and being unaware of how badly underfunded they are. I predict the first annual statement received with the new revised projections will be a big shock. Hopefully, however there will be enough time and warning for many to take action to resolve the gap in their retirement finances.

To help illustrate just how big this gap could be, let's take a simple sum of £10,000 with a compound interest rate of 2% and 5% applied over 16 years. At the end of Year 16 the £10,000 with 2% compound growth rate per year will be worth £13,459, yet the same amount achieving a 5% compound growth rate will be worth £20,789, i.e. 54% more. I think you'll agree this is a significant difference.

We've already discussed the impact of the Total Expense Ratio on your overall Fund performance and this becomes even more critical when your Fund Value is lower than expected, as no–one wants to lose a further large chunk of their fund.

It is important you understand how to read fund data so can make informed business decisions. Below are a few helpful hints.

i. Firstly, when assessing the performance of a Mutual fund ideally you require ten years of performance data. This time period is likely to cover a mix of market conditions, so will translate into a more reliable long–term indicator of a fund's investment management abilities. (the absolute minimum is 5 years data).

ii. As a general rule Fund literature and the financial press report performance without adjusting for sales charges (fees). So be aware of this.

iii. Understand how the investment return has been calculated i.e. whether the annualised investment returns have been calculated using the arithmetic mean, known as the 'simple average', or geometric average known as 'compound average'.

I know this is a bit like a maths lesson, but please keep reading as the difference between the two 'averages', can make a significantly impact on results.

The compound average gives the best reflection of the economic reality of an investment. Why? Let's take an example

Imagine you have an investment plan that has provided you with the following total returns over a six year period.

- Year 1   15%
- Year 2   –8%
- Year 3   22%
- Year 4   4%
- Year 5   –10%
- Year 6   2%

Simple Average   4.17%

The Simple Average would be calculated by adding all the numbers together and dividing by the number of entries (which in this case is six). This gives a Simple

Average of 4.17%. So on this basis if you had invested £100 at the beginning of Year 1 your money would be worth £127.75 at the end of Year 6.

Or would it?

Unfortunately, the simple average makes no allowance for movement upwards or downwards, so does not provide an accurate measure of performance. To achieve this we need to use the Compound Average.

Taking the same figures the compound average equates to only 3.54% growth per year. So the end value of your £100 in Year 6 would be only £123.23

For clarity, the Simple Mean answers the question: *'over a particular number of periods, what was the return of an average year, or what was the return for a typical year?'*
The Compound Average however answers the important question: *'over a particular number of periods, what was the average compound return per year?'*

'What did you actually earn per year on average, compounded annually?'
Because of the way it is calculated the Simple Average will always be bigger than the Compound Average, and so is often used to provide optimistic performance.

You may question why this is an issue, because the difference in our example isn't that much, but increase the fund size, the length of time and the degree of volatility of the market and it can become significantly more pronounced.

The hint therefore is always to check you are reviewing performance based on a Compound Average, as this will provide you with a far more accurate and realistic reflection of performance.

iv.   Remember to allow for inflation. Pensions World (March 2012) stated *"over the last five years UK pension funds achieved a median return of 4.1% a year, which represents a real rate of return of 0.7% a year against the Retail Price Index..."*

0.7% 'actual growth' compared to 4.1% is a big difference, so inflation shouldn't be forgotten.

The performance of the Stock Market, the Fund Manager and the Total Expense Ratio are critical factors in determining the size of your Pension fund when you retire. However with a Defined Contribution Pension that is not the end, there is a final decision which will determine the pension income received, for the rest of your life.

At retirement you have two options, either:

- Buy an Annuity, or
- Take a Drawdown.

The majority of retirees buy an Annuity with their saved pension pot. This involves taking your Fund out of the Stock Market and converting it to a type of insurance policy which provides a monthly income. Once converted, the Annuity cannot be changed and the retiree is locked in for the remainder of their life.

The Drawdown option leaves the money vested in the Stock Market, and therefore still exposed to fluctuations. Lump sums are drawn down to live on. Some retirees follow the Drawdown method before ultimately converting to an Annuity, however to be allowed to follow this option you must have a large pension pot (i.e. Over £100,000).

(The limit is set as over £100,000 – although as we already know from our example with David, a fund of £100,000 doesn't amount to much).

As almost everyone ultimately moves to an Annuity, we will concentrate on this option.

So what is an Annuity?

As already explained, an Annuity is an insurance policy which pays out for your remaining life. The annuity rate is an interest rate set at the time you purchase the annuity, and applied to your pension pot to calculate the annual income you will receive.

With annuities the more guarantees you require concerning how long the policy will pay, and to whom, the lower the rate paid. Put simply the Insurance Company is betting on how long you will live, and whether they need to pay anyone else following your demise. As a result, bizarrely, if you have always kept yourself 'fit and healthy' you will be penalised. Those with ill health can be 'rewarded' with higher Annuity Rates, because statistically they are going to die earlier.

So now that you understand your retirement income is influenced by two key parameters, and we have already established that one of them, the Stock Market, hasn't done particularly well over the last decade – how have Annuity Rates faired in these tough economic times against a Stock Market which has been lacklustre?

7. The Catastrophic Impact of Quantitative Easing

Before we discuss the actual Annuity Rates, it would be good to consider some factors that have influenced their performance.

Usually, if a Government is trying to increase the activity in an economy they achieve this by cutting interest rates. Lower interest rates mean more money in your pocket and this encourages spending, and correspondingly lower interest being paid on deposit accounts also means there is no incentive to save.

The lowering of interest rates commenced in October 2008, when rates were dropped from 5% to 4.5%. The following 5 months saw the rates continue to drop which stimulated some activity and eased the credit crunch slightly but its impact was not strong enough to boost the severely damaged economy, so the Bank of England took the unprecedented decision to do something it had never done before, pump money directly into the economy via Quantitative Easing (QE).

The first round of QE was introduced in March 2009 at the same time as dropping the interest rate to 0.5%. Then between the months of March and November 2009 there was a total injection of £200 billion via QE Programmes. To date there have been five waves of QE within the UK, totalling £375 billion of additional money entering circulation.

The Bank of England pumped this money into the economy by buying financial assets, particularly Government and Corporate Bonds. These were bought using money which had been electronically created (but the effect is the same as literally printing the money).

The institutions selling the bonds (i.e. Commercial Banks or Insurance Companies) received 'new money' into their accounts. This increased money supply meant they were able to lend more proactively, therefore boosting the economy as a whole. In addition, the increased demand for Government Bonds pushed up their value, making them more expensive and a less attractive investment so companies selling the bonds were encouraged to invest elsewhere rather than buy more bonds.

Unfortunately as with all things, one person's gain is another person's loss! So the economy as a whole has benefitted but who have been the major losers of these QE programmes?

Typically, one of the most hard hit communities are those nearing retirement, as the QE programmes have pushed up the price of Gilts (Government Bonds). This has meant the relationship between the price of Gilts and their yield has fallen, as Gilts pay a fixed rate of interest. As pension providers invest in bonds this has put them under increased pressure to maintain Annuity Rates at a healthy level. As you can imagine this has been extremely challenging and, as figures produced by the Better Retirement Group show, simply impossible. It is estimated that Annuity Rates have fallen by over 24% since 2008.

Add to this the influx of overseas money into the UK (as we are considered a Safe Haven in the European Crisis) and Gilt prices have been pushed up even higher.

The devastating effect of this on Pension funds has, however, not simply been restricted to Defined Contribution Schemes, as Final Salary (Defined Benefit) Schemes have also taken a battering, as they must guarantee the returns to their members.

At the end of March 2013 there were 6,316 Defined Benefit schemes in the Pension Protection Fund (PPF) and of these 5,080 (80.4%) were in deficit, to a massive tune of £236.6bn. And this was despite Britain's Top 100 firms having injected £12.7bn into their Pension schemes to bridge the funding gap. This massive negative swing is based on the fact that the cost of paying Final Salary pensions is calculated on the assumption that all assets are invested in bonds. Falling yields require more stock to be held to generate the same level of pension income, so as a result many employers will be presented with a very big bill to support their pension scheme.

It's little wonder that so many Final Salary schemes have been shut in recent years, as employers try to regain control and limit their financial exposure.

Unfortunately, however, if you are a member of a Defined Contribution scheme there is no Company picking up the pieces, all the pain is felt by you the individual.

And given the on–going financial pressures on the economy and the continued risk of the Euro–zone imploding it is not predicted that Annuity Rates will rally in the short term.

Why is this so painful?

We have already discussed Life Expectancy and the table over the page, shows total life expectancy based on current age.

You will notice the older you get, the longer you live e.g. at age 65 years life expectancy is 84 years but once this has been reached you would be expected to live until age 91 years.

Figure 6

Life Expectancy for Men and Women				
	Male		**Female**	
Age	**Years**	**Months**	**Years**	**Months**
65	18	11	22	0
66	18	0	21	1
67	17	2	20	2
68	16	3	19	3
69	15	5	18	5
70	14	7	17	7
71	13	10	16	9
72	13	1	15	11
73	12	4	15	2
74	11	7	14	5
75	10	11	13	8
76	13	3	12	11
77	9	8	12	3
78	9	1	11	7
79	8	6	11	0
80	8	0	10	5
81	7	6	9	10
82	7	0	9	3
83	6	7	8	9
84	6	2	8	3
85	5	10	7	9
86	5	5	7	4
87	5	1	6	11
88	4	9	6	6
89	4	6	6	2
90	4	3	5	9

Source: Tables produced by the Continuous Mortality Investigation Bureau in 1999

Why is this?

Because, having reached 84 years, statistically you then move into the group which outlives the average – hence you gain an additional seven years. Whether you make all seven years or even longer, the underlying message is clear, your pension money needs to last for many years.

The reality of lower Annuity Rates is demonstrated by the example of a non–smoking male of 65 with a pension pot equivalent to £100,000 who was able to secure a pension income of around £17,000 in 1979. Today the same value of pension savings would only deliver a pension of around £5,800. So for every year of retirement our male would be worse off by £11,200 i.e. have an income which is 66% lower, even though he has contributed the same amount into his pension. Imagine if our man lived for 19 years after retiring, he would receive a total of £212,800 less! Significant!

QE and Inflation

Dr. Ros Altmann, an expert on pensions policy, investment banking, savings and retirement and Director General of Saga, was recently quoted as saying in the House of Commons Treasury Committee report on QE (January 2013) that around 95% of annuities have no inflation protection, so these pensioners become poorer over time.

This impact of inflation is demonstrated by taking £50K today at 4% compound inflation. In 20 years you would need an income of approximately £110K, and more than £160K in 30 years to maintain the same level of purchasing power and standard of living.

So why is this so devastating for pensioners?

Because more than 90% of those currently buying annuities choose 'level income' in order to get the higher starting value. But these annuities have no protection against inflation so their purchasing power will reduce each and every year. A sad state of affairs.

There is no doubt that the QE programmes have damaged Annuity Rates and on the Bank's own estimates have also influenced inflation, with the threat of hyperinflation at some point in the future.

Historically within the UK we have had two major indices used to measure our cost of living. The Retail Price Index (RPI) introduced in the 1950's and the Consumer Price Index (CPI), introduced in 1990.

Needless to say RPI remains the highest index standing at 3.3% in June 2013, with CPI at 2.9%.

But are the changes in indices important to pensioners? Yes, because in the Budget of June 2010, Tax Credits, certain Benefits and Public Sector Pensions were changed so that from April 2011 they would increase in line with CPI and not RPI. This policy was then expanded to include additional elements in 2012.

Looking back to 1996 the cumulative inflation rate under RPI equates to 53.6%, whereas CPI only represents 35.6% (April 1996 to April 2011). This means a pensioner retiring in 1996 whose pension was uplifted by RPI would today be 13% better off than a pensioner starting on a similar income but only being uplifted in–line with CPI.

In addition, pensioners have been affected by inflation which has continually been higher than the Government's 2% target and is likely to continue to be so for some time.

8. What if you have Money in the Bank?

The Bank of England reviews the Base Rate each month which influences not only the amount we pay for our mortgages but also the money we receive as interest for money saved in a bank or building society. These organisations make their profit by lending money out for mortgages/loans at a higher rate than they pay 'savers', so a drop in Base Rates is great for home owners but not good news for those who have diligently saved.

In March 2009 the Bank of England dropped the Base Rate to 0.5% and it has remained at this level for the last 4 years.

This rate is deliberately being held low to help prop up the economy and boost activity by putting more money into our pockets, but savers are being penalised.

In 2009 the annual average return on savings dropped to 2.75%. 2010 saw a small rise to 2.85% before dropping back to 2.75% in 2011. High yielding accounts could earn slightly more but they offer this by restricting access to the money. 2010 represented the start of a catastrophic period for savers as the relationship between inflation and interest paid swung to the inverse, i.e. inflation was running higher than the interest being paid. This meant that for savers the spending power of their savings was quite simply being eroded each and every month.

During 2012 inflation stabilized but, when you have taken tax into account, in most instances savers will continue to have the value of their money eroded. And as most forecasts predict interest rates will stay low for several more years, this penalising of savers is not likely to change in the short–term.

Summary of Section One

Below are the key facts you are faced with as you try to plan for your retirement:

- The State Pension introduced in 1909 is overstretched and may be unable to support all the pensioners.

- The UK currently has a population of 56 million which is predicted to increase to 73.2 million by 2035.

- Over the last decade, the UK Stock Market has averagely returned a growth rate of a little less than 7%.

- Of the current UK workforce of 29.3 million, only 14.6 million are making any contribution to a pension.

- Defined Benefit schemes are being closed, as companies look to reduce their financial exposure.

- Defined Contribution schemes offer no guarantees on the income you will receive in retirement.

- From October 2012, Auto Enrolment offered an extremely low start to saving for retirement, for many it could end up being too little too late.

- The UK's £375bn of Quantitative Easing has propped up the economy, but it has been at the expense of reducing Gilt yields.

- Reduced Gilt yields have impacted Annuity Rates which have fallen 24% over the last 5 years.

- The average pension payable to a man aged 65 years with a pension pot of £30,000 is only £1,115 per annum.

- Savings in the bank are not even retaining their purchasing power but are being eroded by inflation as the interest paid on deposits is so low.

- Existing pensioners are being impacted by the higher rates of inflation as their level incomes are required to stretch further.

Having understood all this, what can you do to improve your situation and lessen the impact of the current economic meltdown on your retirement?

What actions can you take to protect your future and take back personal control? Is it possible for you to utilise the current economic situation to your advantage and enhance your future?

We will review this in Section Two.

Section Two

The Advantages and Strengths of Property Investment

9. The Solution to your Pension Shortfall

My aim in this book is to help you understand the extent of the issues which are conspiring against you. As the first generation to be affected by not only the Stock Market performance but also reduced Annuity Rates, you need to understand how the jigsaw fits together. Only by bringing all of these elements together can you fully understand the magnitude of the challenge faced – and how perilously your golden retirement hangs in the balance.

Once you have embraced the situation I believe you have two choices:

1. Remain within your comfort zone and stick your head in the sand hoping it will all sort itself out, or

2. Take control and act proactively to secure your retirement.

If you choose Option 2 and want to implement actions which will be the antidote to your personal retirement crisis, I believe you should seek a solution which ultimately takes each of the variables we have discussed and turns them on their head.
i.e.
1. Is unaffected by fluctuations in the stock market
2. Doesn't involve buying an Annuity
3. Benefits from a growing population
4. Benefits from an ageing population
5. Has the ability to be inflation proof
6. Offers tax efficiencies – just like a pension
7. Is income generating from Day 1
8. Allows you to control and minimise your exposure to risk
9. Enables you to continue to utilize expert help when appropriate

Any investment has a risk and reward balance. When looking at investment from the viewpoint of retirement you need to assess where that balance sits, based on your own personal circumstances. The aim is to reduce risk while increasing the probability of reward. As our current mix of economic factors presents a truly lethal concoction, those looking to secure their future are going to have to take some 'bold but measured' actions.

Doing nothing really isn't an option. In the cold harsh light of day you need to understand that unless you have a Final Salary Pension your retirement years could stretch out as a very miserable existence indeed.

It's key that you accept that additional funds <u>must</u> be invested to fill this gap.

So the question is, how much do you need to commit to your future and where do you invest so you can counter–balance the negative issues?

For all the pressure pensions are currently under don't forget your pension offers distinct benefits regarding tax efficiencies plus employer's contributions, if you are in a company scheme. I believe strongly that you **should not stop** contributing to your occupational pension. If you are contributing to a Personal Pension your focus should be on taking professional advice to ensure you are maximizing your investments, minimising your charges and squeezing every ounce of benefit into your Pension Fund.

The extra actions you need to take now should be in addition to maintaining your pension and you should follow an investment strategy which complements your pension by offering maximum opportunity for reward, while being able to minimise your exposure to risk.

Differentiate

'Investment wisdom begins with the realization that it's the decades, not days that matter. And over the long term diversification really does protect your portfolio' William J Bernstein CNN Money 1st April 2009

My recommendation is to 'differentiate' but when I refer to differentiation I don't mean across different shares, I mean across different Asset Classes. To achieve this it's important that you understand there are four asset classes and each is distinguished by three factors:–

    i.   The historic level of return that asset class has delivered
    ii.   The historic level of risk that asset class has experienced
    iii.   The level of correlation between the investment performance of each asset class.

To my mind, the third factor is the most important as it identifies the independence of each Asset Class. When one class is affected positively or negatively what influence, if any, does it have on the others?

For the last 20–30 years there have been four recognised core asset classes. They are:

    i.   Equities
    ii.   Gilts
    iii.   Cash
    iv.   Property

Currently your pension sits across Asset Classes 1 and 2 – Equities, because pension savings are invested in shares and Gilts because they determine Annuity Rates. The reason why the pain being felt at the moment is so deep is because both of these classes, though independent of each other, have been affected simultaneously by the economy and the dramatic actions the Government has taken.

To me, even with the current Stock Market rally, investing additional money into either of these asset classes at this current time could ring of 'putting good money after bad'. For example, if you were to invest further money into the Stock Market via shares you are still playing in the same Asset Class as your existing pension. Investing in multiple sectors of the same Asset Class (e.g. I'm in 'Technology' and 'Food shares') is a very common mistake and can leave individuals with a warped view of their true exposure.

As diversification is focused on reducing your risk while increasing your opportunity for reward, you need to protect your retirement by investing outside of either of these two classes. This leaves Cash and Property as options to address your pension shortfall.

Unfortunately, as we have already seen 'Cash' is also suffering. So having considerable money on cash deposits is not a solution to fill your pension gap. But what about Cash ISA's? Unfortunately these are also suffering at the hands of inflation, and in February 2013, Citywire.co.uk stated there was only one Cash ISA provider offering an interest rate above inflation – all be it minimally above!

So now to 'Property'

The question is can Property investment offer you a powerful solution to your pension shortfall?

The remainder of this book will be focused on candidly assessing whether investing in property has the ability to plug your pension gap and secure your future. We will look at this from the perspective of you finding yourself in a similar situation to David, who you met earlier in this book. That is:

i.   You are in your late 40s – early 50s, so only have a limited number of years to address your pension shortfall before you wish to retire.

ii. You've realised your pension is insufficient to support you, and you are worried about the gap.

iii. You've always considered Property Investment to be a highly risky option, so you need to be convinced that property is the right solution for you.

As a reminder however, before we go on to talk about Property Investment as a potential solution, it is imperative you understand I am not proposing that you cease investing in your existing pension. A pension does allow you to maximize your savings via tax benefits and employer's contributions (if you are in a company scheme). So even allowing for its current performance you would, in my view, be foolish to sever all ties with this option in favour of other ways to safeguard your retirement.

Remember, we are looking for a way to build strength into your pension position.

The message is clear:

'A pension scheme forms a valuable building block for your retirement, but in today's world one block is insufficient – you need a strategy which has multiple building blocks for stability and security'

So Why Property?

Having understood that Property represents a different asset class to Stocks, Gilts and Cash we now need to consider whether it can deliver for pension purposes.

Before we review the physical calculations let's assess the strength of Property as an investment vehicle to fill your pension shortfall by reviewing its performance against each of the ten issues we have already identified. This will allow you to make an informed decision with all the facts on the table.

Can property investment provide the ultimate pension solution by offering the following characteristics:

1. Be unaffected by fluctuations in the Stock Market?
2. Not require you to buy an annuity?
3. Benefit from a growing population?
4. Benefit from an ageing population?
5. Have the ability to be inflation proof?
6. Offer tax efficiencies?
7. Utilise income today for a stronger retirement?
8. Offer control and minimise exposure to risk?
9. Be able to utilize expert help when appropriate?

We shall take each area in turn.

1. Be unaffected by fluctuations in the Stock Market?

We have just explained that the Housing Market sits in a different Asset Class to the Stock Market, but how can this be when both have experienced a tremendously challenging time over the last few years?

Let's look at what caused the Housing Market to re–adjust in 2008.

In the run up to the Credit Crunch in 2007/2008 both the US and UK followed an approach which allowed lenders of residential mortgage backed securities to package them up and sell them on with the promise of a supposedly low risk investment, with strong returns. However, at that time many of the people who had taken out mortgages had done so when credit was easy and the questions asked by the lender were minimal.

The first sign of problems appeared in the USA, as thousands of families defaulted on their mortgages. (These were families who really should never have been encouraged to have a mortgage). As they defaulted it became apparent that the debt which had been sold on was not of A1 quality. This meant those who bought the debt expecting to receive a guaranteed income were left 'carrying the can' and feeling the pain.

This sub–prime crisis erupted in the US in the summer of 2007, as the residential mortgage backed securities market that had driven the massive growth in credit for home loans prior to 2007 essentially dried up.

As American banks became under increasing financial pressure, and Fannie Mae and Fannie Mac (American Banks) collapsed we realised for the first time in the UK just how interlinked our banking systems had become and how we were one global market. The pain spread to the UK, as we too were guilty of over– zealous lending.

Northern Rock collapsed and was subsequently nationalised and Bradford and Bingley had major problems, as did the other banks which had fuelled the buy–to–let and residential boom. As the banks were suddenly fearful of huge losses they began to dramatically cut back on mortgage lending and so began a vicious circle. The more the banks cut back on lending and demanded higher deposits, the fewer homebuyers could secure finance, the more property prices fell and banks became even more fearful and cut back further on their lending.

The property market has a massive impact on the UK wealth factor as we have such a high attraction to home ownership. We really do follow the saying 'An Englishman's home is his castle'.

When house prices are increasing we all feel wealthy and many people remortgage money from their home to spend on consumer items boosting consumer spending.

When house prices fall suddenly this is not possible and those who had over–geared themselves (i.e. had high borrowing in relationship to assets) in the good times found themselves pressurised and in negative equity. Many are nervous about investing in property because they fear these very 'crashes'.

However, it is important to understand that the housing market follows a cyclical pattern, and has done throughout history. So moments of strong growth are followed by price corrections. This cyclical pattern is produced when periods of growth go that 'bit too far' and the reins are required to be pulled in slightly. The reason the Credit Crunch hit the UK housing market so fiercely this time around, was in part because the preceding period of growth had been so explosive, so the brakes had to be applied harder.

That being the case however, the chart below (produced from data supplied Nationwide Building Society) illustrates the trend in real house prices since Quarter 1 1975 to Quarter 1 2013. As you can see there is distinct movement throughout this 38 year period, but even allowing for this (and adjusting for inflation) overall the trend in Real House Prices has been a compound growth of circa 2.8% per annum.

Figure 7

Real house prices 1975-2013

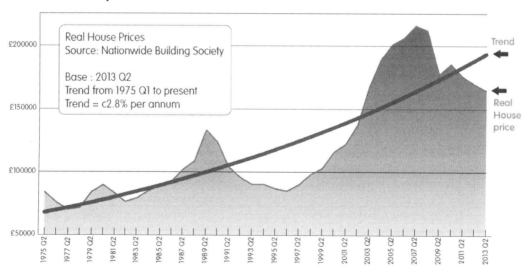

House Prices adjusted for retail prices. This uses the Office for National Statistics Retail Price Index (RPI) to convert nominal prices to current prices. For example, a typical property in 2005 Q1 would, on average, have cost £152,790 at the time. The buy this amount of 'retail goods' today would require £201,123. A smooth trend has been fitted to the real house price series. This trend has been fitted from 1975 Q1 to the latest quarter and is an exponential curve.

Depending on the Property Pension Planning Strategy you adopt, the movement of house prices can become almost insignificant over time. Rental income is the key factor you should be concerned with.

Our obsession as a Nation with capital growth is due to the 'wealth factor' we have described. However, the truth is as a pensioner you feel wealthy when you have money in your pocket to spend. After–all, we can all think of people who are equity rich but cash poor. From a pensioner's viewpoint they are those living in a large house with the mortgage paid off, but unable to afford to heat the house and feed themselves – that for me spells a retirement of misery.

So although house prices have fallen in the last few years the key factor, 'Rental income,' has remained buoyant, and in fact has even seen a corresponding boost as more people have turned to renting unable to secure lending to purchase their own home.

Under the law of supply and demand this has actually caused rental prices nationwide to rise in value and even allowing for the new Government incentives; Funding for Lending and the Government Backed Mortgages it is projected the requirement for rental properties will remain, as people need homes and our population is expanding dramatically. Refer back to Figure 4, Page 29 if you need to remind yourself of the extent of population growth we are facing.

From a long term investment perspective the current lower house prices are in fact highly attractive, as the Gross Rental Yields achieved on the property are consequently higher. The Gross Rental Yields and subsequent Net Rental Yields are critical for pension planning purposes, as they represent the money a retiree will receive.

As you can see none of this activity in the housing market is as the result of Stock Market confidence. In fact, having a buoyant rental market simultaneously with a struggling Stock Market is proof their correlation is low. Wise investment in Property, therefore, really can offer a retirement planning safe haven outside of the Stock Market.

2. Not require you to buy an annuity

As we are already aware, the value of your pension pot is determined by the Stock Market performance over the period of saving. This saved money is then used at retirement to buy an annuity which provides a monthly income. 'Annuity Rates' are quoted as a percentage and are applied to the saved pension pot to calculate the monthly income to be paid.

There are different choices of annuity and up until December 2012 the rates for men and women were different. (Female annuity rates were lower as their life expectancy is longer). Now, however, under the European Law of Gender Equalisation the rates for both genders are the same.

As we are already aware the annuity calculation is influenced by the yield on Gilts, but on top of this the Insurance provider applies additional risk and exposure factors. In simple terms, to an insurance company the higher the probability of you living longer and needing to be supported by your retirement income, the more financial liability you represent to them, and so the lower their annuity rate.

As an example the following all reduce the annuity rate paid:

    i   Inflation linking or an income which is escalating each year.

    ii   Including a spouse so they continue to receive a percentage of your pension income following your death.

    iii   Guaranteeing that your pension income will be paid for a defined period (e.g. five years) even if you were to die on Day 2 of your retirement.

    iv   Your postcode – yes where you live really does affect your retirement income.

As you might expect the world of Annuities has its own terminology. To help explain the different options here are the key terms used.

Single Life – This means the pension income is only payable to the named individual on the policy. Upon their death, whether this is on Day 1 of their retirement or twenty years later, the pension payments cease. Any surviving spouse will need to provide for themselves under their own policy.

Joint Life 50% – On the death of the named policy holder, 50% of the pension income will continue to be paid to the named spouse. (Figures quoted on websites are normally on the basis of the male being three years older than the female – so if your relationship does not match this standard formula then the annuity calculations will change slightly to profile the risk to the insurer). Likewise, if you require a greater percentage of the income to continue for your spouse, e.g. 75% then the annuity rates will also be amended (downwards) to reflect this.

Level – The pension income will remain at a constant level throughout the period it's being paid. Long term this is a far less costly/ risky option for the pension provider so the annuity paid is initially higher. 90% of existing pensioners are attracted to this option! However, all the risk lays with the pensioner, as the payment does not increase at any point over the term of the pension to compensate for inflation. This means over the period of the retirement the pensioner gets poorer as every single year passes.

Consequently, as the years pass the pensioner is more likely to be worrying about stretching his finances to make ends meet. For example: with an initial pension income of £5,857 per annum (the rate as at the 11th April 2013 for a Single Life, No Guarantee Pension, based on a pension size of £100,000) and inflation at 2.94% (the average inflation figure over the 15 years between December 1997 – November 2012. Source Office of National Statistics) the purchasing power of a Level pension would drop significantly over a 18 year period.

You may be surprised by how much the table below demonstrates the erosive effect of inflation.

Figure 8

The Loss of Spending Power due to Inflation at 2.94%			
Year	Value Of Pension in Real Terms	Year	Value Of Pension in Real Terms
1	£5,857	10	£4,478
2	£5,685	11	£4,346
3	£5,518	12	£4,218
4	£5,355	13	£4,094
5	£5,198	14	£3,974
6	£5,045	15	£3,857
7	£4,897	16	£3,744
8	£4,753	17	£3,633
9	£4,613	18	£3,527

Since the life expectancy of a 65 year old man is 83 years, by the end of this additional 18 years of life the purchasing power of his pension would be equivalent to £3,527 pa today, or a measly £293 per month. This equates to a 40% drop in the spending power. Imagine the pain for current pensioners when the rate of inflation was running at 5%+.

Inflation is particularly vicious for pensioners as a large percentage (9%) of their annual spend is on utilities such as fuel, water and electricity. Here the costs are outside their control. A recent report by retirement specialist LV (published in March 2012) revealed that retirees in the UK had in–fact experienced a 33% increase in living costs since the year 2000.

RPI – The pension income is uplifted annually in line with inflation as measured by the Retail Price Index. RPI runs at a higher rate than the Consumer Price Index and, by many, is considered a more accurate reflection of the true cost of living.

3% Escalation – This option applies a fixed escalation irrespective of the actual underlying inflation occurring in the country. If inflation is running below 3% you feel wealthy; however anything above 3% and your spending power is still eroded.

Interestingly, the annuity values shown below, show the payment of an RPI tracked annuity is lower than the 3% escalation option. As annuity rates are calculated by actuaries based on probabilities and financial exposure of the pension provider we can read into this that RPI is currently projected to run at a higher level than 3%, even though the Governments inflationary target is 2%. Is this the pension provider hedging against the further impact of the QE?

Figure 9

Income Per Annum at Age 65	
Single Life, Level ,No Guarantee	£5,857
Single Life, Level, 5yr Gurantee	£5,838
Single Life, RPI, 5 yr Guarantee	£3,516
Single Life, 3% Escalation, 5 yr Guarantee	£4,073
Joint Life 50%, Level, No Guarantee	£5,278
Joint Life 50%, 3% Escalation, No Guarantee	£3,538

Based on £100,000 pension – Hargreaves Lansdown 11th April 2013

Guarantee – The Guarantee kicks in from the commencement of the policy and normally runs for 5 years, but may be up to 10 years. The guarantee ensures the annuity will continue to pay an income, even if the named policyholder dies during the guarantee period. After this period payments cease on death.

Holding off converting your income to an annuity until you are older offers a better return. However, you run the risk that annuity rates continue to drop in the interim, or the value of your Fund still vested in the Stock Market drops in value. So you may in–fact be no better off.

So why does investing in Property represent such a strong solution to a Pension Shortfall?

The size of your pension pot and your choice of annuity can both have a dramatic impact on the income you receive each month. However, Property investment does not require you to buy an annuity, with property your income is determined by the market rental value, which is affected in the main by two factors, neither of which are Stock Market or Annuity Rate related.

These are:

  i.   Supply and demand for property
  ii. Affordability of rental income versus wages

Supply and Demand – The more people there are looking for accommodation in a specific area, the higher the rental value will be.

Renting has gathered increasing momentum over the years as the tightening of credit by the banks has made it difficult for some to afford to purchase a property. The high cost of living, combined with the large deposits (20%–25%) demanded by mortgage companies has made getting onto the housing ladder challenging. Even with the Governments new Funding for Lending Scheme and the 'Help to Buy' Scheme, there are still tight criteria to determine the affordability and those who don't meet the criteria, but want their own home, rent.

Once renting, however, it is even more difficult to save the required deposit. So those who rent can easily slip into becoming 'life time renters'. (Remember affordability of residential homes is based on salary income, and committed outgoings).

The Press has even quoted that the UK is moving towards being a nation of 'renters', with the average age of a First Time Buyer (who has no help from the Bank of Mum and Dad) increasing to nearly 40 years, while those with parental help are managing to make the first steps onto the ladder aged 28 – 29 years. There are now a total of 8.5million people renting their accommodation.

Affordability of Rental Income v Wages – Rental income will be affected by affordability versus wages. Although not perfectly matched, the balance between these two elements has always stayed more or less in line.

This ability for rents to rise in relation to inflationary wage rises is a fundamental strength of property investment as it means the purchasing power of the rental income can be maintained long term.

As we know the pension income you receive is based on the value of your pension pot and the current annuity rate at the time of your retirement. Unless you are in a company pension and your employer has been contributing the value of your pot will be determined solely by the performance of the money you have personally contributed (plus tax benefits).

With rental income however you are able to leverage your money in two ways to build your pension. Firstly, by receiving 100% of the Gross Rental figure and not just for the 25% of the property which actually belongs to you (i.e. you put in 25% deposit only). Secondly, by building an asset base where the mortgage debt is being paid for by someone else, i.e. your tenant.

This concept of 'leverage' is fundamental in building retirement wealth, as it allows you to make your money go further. Importantly, investing in Property for your retirement gives you an asset base which has the capacity to pump out rental income month on month, year on year; which has the ability to stay in line with inflation and can be passed to a surviving spouse / family members when you die.

And because property can be inherited you can be assured that the effort you put into investing today will not only be for your own benefit but also for future generations of your family. A scenario which is completely impossible with an annuity based retirement income.

3. Benefit from a Growing Population

As we've seen the overall UK population is growing. The effect on housing demand as a consequence is not linear however, as not only is the population growing but the demographics and housing requirements are changing. Gone are the days when people lived at home until they were married and divorce was rare.

The housing stock is under increased pressure in the UK as we accommodate the cultural shifts of:

- Moving away from parents and having your own home before getting married.

- Marrying later in life.

- Divorce and separation increasing the requirement for two houses, where once there was one. In 2011, 42% of marriages ended in divorce – a total of 117,558.

Also, as a nation we are way behind the required number of houses to accommodate our expanding population. The UK needs to be building 300,000 new homes per year (as quoted by a study by the Future Homes Commission, October 2012). However, with the financial crisis and subsequent recession we have failed to meet these figures and in 2010/11 the number of new homes built was just 121,200. Even though the Government has now put incentives in place to encourage building to re–commence, meeting the housing need in the short term is unrealistic.

After–all there is a considerable time lag between the 'agreement to build' and having the end home ready for occupation, due to legal complexities, planning permission, labour availability, build times, etc.

Also as council house stock has been sold off and Housing Associations are unable to accommodate everyone seeking a home, the requirement for private landlords to fill the void is likely to increase. For example, the Unitary Authority of Nottingham has circa 12,000 families on its waiting list.

(Data from https://www.gov.uk/government/statistical–data–sets/live–tables–on–rents–lettings–and–tenancies)

While the growing population places additional burden on the country and State benefits, it is a key success factor in rental property. Under the law of supply and demand it is likely, both house prices and, importantly, rental values will increase as more people seek accommodation.

So the next question is *"does Property investment also offer a solution to the ageing population?"*

4. Benefit from an Ageing Population

The ageing population continues to increase housing demands, as unlike other cultures, we don't have older family members living with younger generations within the same home.

The chart (Figure 4) on page 29 illustrated that in 2010 14.1m of the population were over 60 years old. And according to the latest Laing and Buisson survey (2013), there are 431,500 elderly and disabled people in residential care (including nursing), approximately 414,000 of whom are aged 65+. So this means that over 95% of care home residents are aged 65 or over. The rest of the elderly are still living in their own homes.

As people are living longer this puts more pressure on housing stock and it would not surprise me if in years to come more elderly people downsize and move into rented accommodation. The anticipation of many years of retirement stretching out in front of them with little regular income and all their equity tied up in their home will be no fun.

Many will be forced to utilise the capital within their home as living expenses, either via selling and then renting, or taking out a Lifetime Mortgage where the debt remains outstanding until such time as the house is sold on death, and the interest rolls up. This will be covered in Chapter 29 'Property Investment Pitfalls to Avoid'.

5. Have the ability to Be Inflation Proof

Over time Property investment offers you the ability and flexibility to increase your rental income to reflect inflationary rises, which means you are able to protect your income.

Protection of your retirement income is however only one side of the inflationary benefits offered by investing in Property. Over time, inflation can erode the spending power of your money – a negative scenario – but can have a highly beneficial effect as it also erodes the value of your debt.

With a mortgage the amount of money (capital) you need to repay remains constant (assuming you do not remortgage and release additional capital during the term) but the 'real value' of this money reduces every year by inflation. This is why mortgage investment debt is classified as 'Good Debt' as you can leverage your tenant and inflation to pay it down.

To see an example of the power of inflation on the 'real value' of your mortgage debt refer to the table overleaf (Figure 10) where mortgages of £60,000 and £120,000 have been subjected to inflation at a rate of 2.94%.

When it comes to paying off the mortgages at the end of the 25 Year term (assuming Interest Only Mortgages) the value outstanding will still be £60,000 and £120,000 respectively, but to clear these debts will take the equivalent of £29,317 and £58,634 in today's money. The compounding effect of inflation at 2.94% has eroded 51.1% of the Debt's Value.

Figure 10

Real Value' of Mortgage Debt with inflation at 2.94%		
End of Year	**Mortgage Debt**	
1	£60,000	£120,000
2	£58,236	£116,472
3	£56,524	£113,048
4	£54,862	£109,724
5	£53,249	£106,498
6	£51,684	£103,367
7	£50,164	£100,328
8	£48,689	£97,379
9	£47,258	£94,516
10	£45,868	£91,737
11	£44,520	£89,040
12	£43,211	£86,422
13	£41,941	£83,881
14	£40,708	£81,415
15	£39,511	£79,021
16	£38,349	£76,698
17	£37,222	£74,443
18	£36,127	£72,255
19	£35,065	£70,130
20	£34,034	£68,069
21	£33,034	£66,067
22	£32,062	£64,125
23	£31,120	£62,240
24	£30,205	£60,410
25	**£29,317**	**£58,634**
Value of Debt Eroded	£30,683	£61,366
Percentage of Debt Eroded	51.1%	51.1%

To be able to benefit from the full value of this effect, wages need to rise in line with inflation. However even if they are slightly behind the effect will still be significant, particularly if you have the full 25 years (or more) available to you before you want the property to be unencumbered (i.e. with no mortgage outstanding). After–all the longer you can leave it, the lower the 'real value' of the debt will be.

This calculation is produced with an average inflation rate, but as we know inflation can rise and fall on a monthly basis. The Governments' Target is 2% CPI but currently it is running at 2.9% (June 2013) and RPI is at 3.3%.

One of the envisaged side effects of the QE programmes is increased inflation as there is more money available to spend in the economy.

Inflationary rises in consumer items can be hard to tolerate, but from a wealth transfer perspective inflation has an important role to play. The high inflation rates we have seen in recent years (September 2012 – RPI 5.6%, CPI 5.2%) have removed great chunks of mortgage debt and transferred greater wealth to homeowners and property investors. It's the savers who yet again have been the losers in the current economic climate.

Some could even argue that the high inflation we have experienced over the last couple of years has been a deliberate ploy by the Government to reduce their own debt.

In summary, Property investment offers the distinct advantage of having the opportunity to be inflation proof. Both in terms of the rental income received during retirement and also via the erosion of the value of your mortgage debt on route to your retirement.

6. Offer Tax Efficiencies

One highly attractive element of pensions are the tax benefits. As the money you pay into a pension comes from your pay–packet before you are taxed so as a lower rate tax payer for every £100 of pension contribution you make you will only experience a reduction of £80 in your take home pay. For a higher rate tax payer this will be only £60.

In addition, if you are in a company pension scheme your employer not only contributes for you, but you don't pay tax on their contributions either. This certainly represents a powerful pension benefit.

However, before we go to discover if Property investment is able to offer any such tax benefits, it is important to make clear that although the money contributed to a pension is tax free, the income you receive from your annuity is not. In fact, when it comes to retirement all your income pots are added together for tax purposes and you are taxed at the highest level on your taxable income (i.e. your income after allowances). This means you may exceed your personal allowance and be liable for tax. The taxable income rates for 2013/2014 are shown below

Taxable Income	Rate of Tax
£0 – £32,010	20% (basic rate)
£32,011 – £150,000	40% (higher rate)
Over £150,000	45% (additional rate)

So does Property investment offer any tax efficiencies?

Rental income is taxable. However Property does offer the advantage that you are entitled to offset a considerable amount of expenditure and so reduce your tax bill. To ensure you don't pay unnecessary tax I would advise you work closely with your Accountant to ensure you apply all the allowances you are entitled to.

However, to provide you with an overview you may wish to have a look at the Government web–link shown below which provides you with a complete list of the 'Allowable expenses'.

www.gov.uk/renting–out–a–property/paying–tax

As it currently stands, the list is as follows but it is always worth checking the web site to see if there have been any changes.

Allowable Expenses

Allowable expenses are those expenses that are necessary for the day to day running of your property, and include:

- Letting Agent's fees
- Legal fees for lets of a year or less, or for renewing a lease for less than 50 years
- Accountant's Fees
- Buildings and Contents insurance
- Mortgage Interest
- Maintenance and repairs to the property (but not improvements)
- Utility bills, like gas, water and electricity
- Rent, ground rent, service charges

- Council Tax (during refurbishment and any void periods)
- Services you pay for, like cleaning or gardening
- Other direct costs of letting the property, like phone calls, stationery and advertising

Allowable expenses don't include 'capital expenditure' – like buying a property or renovating it beyond repairs to wear and tear.

However the Government introduced the 'Landlord's Energy Saving Allowance' which is a tax allowance with lets landlords claim on their tax return against the cost of buying and installing energy saving items. The maximum tax relief per property is £1,500.

7. Be able to utilise income today to provide for a stronger retirement

One key advantage that Property investment offers is that you can receive rental income each month. Pension income, though contributed pre–tax, is locked away and cannot be accessed until such time as you retire – in other words during the period you are contributing to a pension your money follows a 'one way process'. Property investment on the other hand offers a 'two way process' and allows you to leverage your money immediately.

Wise Property investment is focused on purchasing below current market value and most importantly for 'cash flow', it is this monthly rental cash–flow which is the 'golden goose' as it's like having a salary every month –one for which you have not had to work such long hours.

In the investing world most investment properties are purchased with an Interest Only Mortgage (this is permitted for Buy–To–Let Mortgages even though the residential market has tightened the criteria in this area). Interest Only Mortgages are cheaper, so provide the investor with improved cash–flow, and as the mortgage interest can be offset against revenue, they can appear to be extremely favourable. However their limitation is that the mortgage debt only reduces with inflation. Refer back to Figure 10 page 67 and you will see it takes 25 years to reduce the debt by 51% and it would take over 500 years to reduce the 'real value' of the debt to less than the equivalent of 1p today. So perhaps a little longer than the average person is planning to live. (this is based on inflation at 2.94% pa)

As a long term pension plan it would be advisable to consider very carefully how you can utilise this income received today to help repay your Buy–To–Let lender. All lenders have age restrictions on their lending into retirement. Even if they extend that age limit today there is nothing to stop them reducing it again tomorrow. We will discuss this further in Chapter 13, in the sub–section Financing Your Investment.

8. Offer Control and the ability to minimise your exposure to risk

Maximum investment control and minimum risk is the ultimate goal with any investment, but there is always a balance to strike. Investing in Property has its own risks, but as an investor you have the opportunity to make decisions and take actions which can place more 'balls in your court'. This ability to have increased control over your investment is a fundamental benefit offered by Property.

We have already mentioned a few of these benefits, but to summarise please find over the next few pages a consolidated list of the benefits Property brings to your investment portfolio:

Property is a Tangible Asset – Bricks and mortar can be seen and felt. Unlike equity shares that you never actually see, you can drive down a street and refer to a physical building. As such you can use all available information to understand your financial exposure in any purchase. So, prior to investing your money, you can make informed investment decisions.

Once purchased your investment performance is generated in 'real time', ie you don't have to wait until the Annual Statement is received to understand how things are doing. Your feedback is monthly, which means you can make timely amendments if required, to keep your asset producing a cash return.

In addition, when investing in bricks and mortar you can choose where you invest, whether it is a town or city, whether it is houses or flats etc. You are able to do your own due diligence and choose a location which offers the opportunity for the results you require. In essence, Property allows you to become the owner of your own business, a business which will pay you in retirement. Owning Property provides you with the opportunity to take responsibility for your own old age, rather than leaving your future to the mercy of external forces, whether this is the Stock Market, Gilts or Bonds, a Pension Provider or a Fund Manager. Of course this does also mean the 'buck stops with you' and you can't blame anyone else.

Due Diligence (DD) is the name of the game and there are a myriad of tools, mentorships and educational programmes available to help you, so there really is no excuse for not doing DD thoroughly. Particularly, as much of the initial stages can be completed from the comfort of your own home.

These sites all provide valuable information which can help your decision making:

* www.rightmove.co.uk
* www.zoopla.com
* www.nethouseprice.com

- www.propertynotepad.co.uk
- www.Nestoria.co.uk

With an average mutual fund you have no such opportunity to select where your money is being invested, so you have little ability to complete your own due diligence.

I believe, as a retirement strategy to sit alongside your existing pension you should be looking for the opportunity to control your cash–flow. Investing in Property provides you with range of choices as there are many types of housing stock to choose from including terrace, semi–detached or detached; 1 Bed, 2 Bed, 3 Bed etc. Because you can determine the size, type and value of the Property you can calculate your investment return right from the beginning even prior to parting with your money.

On a personal note, we have tended to move away from investing in flats, (we have just four in our portfolio). Freehold is more attractive to us as it offers greater control for the following reasons:

i. We can control our cost base more tightly, as there are no Service Charges and Ground Rent expenditure over which we have no influence.

ii. There is no requirement to pay to extend short leases. In such a situation the negotiating power sits fairly and squarely with the freeholder.

iii. There is no risk, although unlikely, of an extension not being granted on a short lease. Such a situation would make it nigh on impossible to sell your property and attain a mortgage, and the value of your property would be dramatically impacted.

iv. The property can be held indefinitely and passed as an asset within the family as it will never revert back to the ownership of the freeholder at a future date.

Expanding on the concept of control, you can also invest to attract the type of tenants you desire, whether these are single professionals, families or students.

All of these elements allow you to minimise your financial risk in the future and maximise your rewards.

Property is less Volatile – The housing market is also considered far less volatile than the Stock Market.

Stock prices fluctuate on a daily basis, as they react to influences from the economy, company performance, changes of senior leadership etc. Anything that has the power to affect 'confidence', i.e. the publication of a financial report, or the notification of a

CEO resigning can lead to an instantaneous change in a share value. And the FTSE100 companies are certainly not immune to dramatic changes of fortune.

For example, an investment of £100 in Royal Bank of Scotland in 2002 would have been worth a measly £4 in March 2012, while the same amount put into Lloyds would have been worth just £8. Barclays fared better, but is still down 30% since 2002.

The list below produced by the publication Investment Week, shows the 'Biggest FTSE100 Losers' during the period 4th March 2002 – 3rd March 2012, as you can see several of the falls are highly significant.

Bottom Ten FTSE 100 stocks

Name	% return
Royal Bank of Scotland	–96
Lloyds Banking Group	–92
Wolseley	–49
Barclays	–29
RSA Insurance Group	–28
Capital Shopping Centres	–16
ITV	–15
Aviva	–8
Kingfisher	–6
J Sainsbury	–5

Although the Property Market has its own cycle, it is much slower, which gives you time to think and take necessary action. Also the 'Housing Crashes' we hear of, just like the share prices above are always based on the capital value of the property, rather than the rental income. Rental income is almost completely independent and this is a fundamental advantage. Share dividends, on the other hand, are 100% connected to the performance of the company, and that performance is closely linked to their share price. So even though the underlying property values may fluctuate, your rental income could remain static, or even rise as the factors which influence it are different.

Within Property investment you even have the opportunity to further reduce the volatility of your income by fixing your mortgage payments.

You can Increase the Value of Property – Unlike shareholders as a Property investor you have the ability to directly increase the value of your investment, which means you may be able to increase the rental income received.

To date I have purchased and refurbished a total of 34 houses (either for my own family portfolio or for my investors), each has been purchased below the current market value and has had 'value added' during the refurbishment process. There are a multitude of ways that you can add value to a property, below are some of those most commonly used:

Buy, refurbish and hold – buying a property at a lower price and then refurbishing to achieve a higher value is a fundamental property strategy. I would always recommend you only undertake 'light refurbishments' rather than full structural work, as full structural work can take considerably more time, costs can easily escalate and importantly you don't start receiving your Rental Income until the property is tenanted. With regard to the refurbishment I would also recommend you cost out the work required (ideally with the Trades Person who is going to complete it for you) prior to making your Offer. This way you can have a tight grip on the expenses and minimise your risk of nasty surprises.

Only recently there was an article in the paper about a lady who bought what she thought was her dream cliff top home at an auction. Unfortunately, she did not take time to view the property and ascertain the extent of the work required, even though the auction papers clearly stated 'structurally damaged'. Then, to compound matters, she foolishly chose not to have a survey on the property. One week after purchasing the property for £155k a large portion of the garden fell into the sea, and then at the beginning of March 2013 half of the house fell away also.

This is why it is imperative that you, or someone acting for you, view the property (ideally including the Surveyor), to protect your interests.

Within the strategy 'Buy, Refurbish and Hold' there are several elements you can consider over and above the improvement of the general décor within the property. Below are a few options for consideration:

i.   **Add double glazing** – double glazing is almost considered an essential these days, and houses without it are often marked down in price. If you can purchase the property for a lower value than the cost of upgrading to new windows this could be a quick win.

ii. **Add an extra bedroom** – within the UK we value houses based on the number of bedrooms, rather than the square footage. This means you don't necessarily need to increase the overall living space to achieve an increase in both house value and rental yield. Of course the house needs to lend itself to accommodating an extra room easily, but it can certainly be worth investigating. We ourselves have recently spent under £2,000 converting a property from a 3 bedroom to a 4 bedroom house, which has not only put the house value up but more importantly allowed us to take the Gross Rental Yield to above 13%.

iii. **Add a driveway or garage** – garages and driveways, like bedrooms, also add value to a property. So if there is space to accommodate them without it being detrimental to the property (i.e. it makes the garden too small), they are also worth considering.

In contrast to the above suggestions, there really is nothing you can do as an individual to improve the stock price of Marks & Spencer's, even if you hold a few thousand shares. Proof again that Property investment puts far more options in your hands. Options which could make a massive difference to you when you come to retire.

You Have Direct ownership, which means you have Direct Control – As a property investor, you have direct ownership of your asset and therefore you have control over your own cash generator. It is your decision whether you increase the rent charged so improving your cash–flow. By comparison you don't have the same ability to increase the dividend paid out on a stock!

This is however not your only area of control, as you also have the opportunity:

i. to do your own due diligence and financial analysis.

ii. to vet your tenants and increase your income certainty through Rent Guarantee Schemes, Deposits and Guarantors.

iii. to monitor your investment performance monthly and make necessary changes along the way to maximise the return.

iv. to sell or remortgage the property to release equity as required. Releasing equity will, of course, reduce the cash flow achieved but it will not mean selling the asset altogether. A word or warning though: DO NOT over leverage yourself financially.

v. to retain an asset which can go on producing an income after your death. We already know that when selecting an annuity you need to determine whether your partner should continue to benefit after your death. To do so will reduce the pension income you receive while alive – but with Property, income is retained at 100% in both circumstances.

vi.   In addition, with a pension you have to decide if you want a guaranteed payment for a defined period (ie 5 years), as we know this again reduces the pension you receive in your lifetime. No guarantee and no spousal payment means your pension ceases on your death and the money you have diligently saved into your pension fund is lost. With Property there may be Inheritance Tax to pay but fundamentally the asset does not disappear and family members can benefit long after you have departed this earth.

To put this into perspective much of the family wealth retained in dynastic families comes from the passing of property assets between generations, not pensions. Property is a physical asset which allows you to influence the lives of future generations of your family.

Property as a Diverse Asset Class – We have already covered how Property investment provides the opportunity to invest your money into a different, diverse Asset Class which is not perilously linked to the Stock Market and annuity performance – it keeps the control in your court.

Property allows you to Leverage Your Money – We have also already covered how you can leverage your money via a mortgage. If you purchase wisely for 'cash flow' and start early enough the mortgage payment you make will not exceed 75% of the rental income, and the additional spare income can cover all the property related costs and provide you with a positive return.

Utilising the rental income to reduce your mortgage debt also means you are able to increase your percentage ownership of the property (i.e. equity in the property). So put simply you are able to leverage your tenant to build your retirement wealth.

Try going into a bank and asking for a loan to invest in the Stock Market and I guarantee the response you receive will be different!

You Can Insure Your property, and its Contents – As the owner of an investment property you can insure against circumstances which could take considerable income from your pocket. Unfortunately, if you are choosing to invest additional money into your pension fund to fill your shortfall you don't have the same luxury.

There are several forms of insurance to help protect your property investment?:

i.   **Building Insurance:** As part of the terms of a mortgage you need to have Buildings Insurance, this protects your property from damage resulting from: fire, flood and storms, vandalism, malicious damage or natural disasters (like subsidence). It also covers you for damage from falling trees or vehicles.

All of these could cost you considerable money but buildings insurance ensures you are able to rectify any of these situations, without being severely out of pocket. The reason a Bank requires Buildings Insurance to be 'live' on Exchange of a sale, is because they want to ensure their money is safe, so by default this means your money is safe also.

ii. **Contents Insurance**: even if you rent out a property unfurnished it is wise to have an element of Contents Insurance as this will cover items such as carpets etc. Again providing you financial 'peace of mind'.

iii. **Rent Guarantee Schemes:** These insurance policies are designed to help you evict non–paying tenants, while protecting your rental income. Some policies will even pay 50% of the rent for three months after the successful eviction, while you find new tenants. Such schemes are a great way of protecting your investment during retirement and taking away one of the worries often banded around by 'non investors'.

iv. **Guarantors:** are another way of reducing your financial risk, as the guarantor is responsible for paying whatever they have committed too, should the tenant default.

v. **Deposits:** Ensuring your investment property is reviewed regularly, either by yourself or your Letting Agent is a good way of making sure your property is being looked after. It gives you the ability to provide guidance during the tenancy term to help maintain the quality of your investment. However, at the end of the tenancy a deposit provides you with an insurance policy to cover the cost of 'making good' any areas of the property which are left unsatisfactory. (To be able to fully utilise the value of the deposit, I would recommend that an inventory is completed when the tenants move into the property. This way the opportunity for disputes is greatly reduced). By law, all deposits must be held in an approved Deposit Scheme.

The choice is yours, you have the flexibility to 'mix and match' whichever of these insurance policies you desire, based on your own personal circumstances. The only policy required legally by the mortgage lender is Buildings Insurance.

Property doesn't have to be sold to raise capital – There are two main ways to raise a pension income from your saved pension fund:

- purchase an annuity
- drawdown

Option 1 – as we know, involves purchasing an annuity which is an insurance policy backed by Government bonds and corporate bonds. Annuity rates have fallen dramatically in recent years and are projected to continue to do so, and, once you have purchased your annuity, you are locked in for life (so a big decision that you need to take with care).

Option 2 – a Drawdown is different as you leave your money vested in the Stock Market and just take out a lump sum. There are restrictions on how much money you can extract tax free, and, of course, the concept that the investment remaining in the Stock Market grows in value to replace the amount extracted is risky, for all the reasons we have already discussed.

Both of these options involve you selling some or all of your pension fund to generate your retirement income. In the case of Drawdown you have to be careful not to run out of money (which is one of the reasons this option is not advised for fund values under £100,000).

Investment property offers you the ability to remortgage and release cash which is 'tax–free'. Releasing this money does not involve you having to sell your asset, unlike the conversion of shares to an annuity, or the drawn down option.

A Word of Warning:

If you remortgage money out of your investment property, even though it is tax free, not only does the cash flow reduce (because your mortgage payment will have gone up), but also your debt increases. This of course will require paying back in the future so needs to be considered in your strategy.

That being said, over time there may be the opportunity to release all / most of the initial seed capital and deliver an infinite return on your investment.

In addition, with Property there is no limit to the number of properties you can own. So long as you meet the bank lending criteria you can invest, and certainly you can hold a property indefinitely if unencumbered – there is never the need to sell.

The key word is 'unencumbered'. You may well be required to sell if you have followed an Interest Only investment route and have outstanding debt at the time the Bank rules you 'too old' to remortgage. If you are unable to clear the debt with alternative funds a sale may be forced.

A Repayment Mortgage would negate all this and there would be no requirement for you to sell.

I would recommend – If you wish to follow the Interest Only investment strategy you plan the number of houses you need in your portfolio, so you can sell some and clear the debt on the remaining properties. Don't worry I will cover this in Chapter 20 'How Many Houses will I need'.

Of course the longer you are able to hold the properties the greater the erosional impact inflation will have on the value of the debt, so the less houses you will need to sell to release the required capital. (But don't be fooled you cannot rely on inflation alone, refer back to Figure 10 Page 67 and you will see it takes 25 years to half a mortgage value simply by inflation, assuming inflation is running at a consistent 2.94% pa). It's important you also remember, if you sell a property you will be liable for Capital Gains Tax.

Property investment offers options, so it is your choice which route you follow and whether you will need to sell property. We will discuss the merits of Repayment v Interest Only further in Chapter 13 – which will hopefully help you make your own informed decisions.

9. Be able to receive help implementing the strategy

Taking on and embracing any new investment strategy is naturally daunting and overwhelming. However, in the world of Property investment there are a multitude of individuals / companies who are able to help you on your journey. For example via my mentoring business Alton Property Mentoring, I educate individuals who wish to complete the investing themselves and via my Hands–Free business Alton Property Partners I work with clients who want to contract out the investment work, so they can focus on what is important to them.

Working with someone who has already 'walked the walk' means you can leverage their skills, knowledge and experience to smooth your journey. In addition, with Property investment the support does not stop as soon as you have purchased the property, as you can also utilise the support / skill of a Letting Agent to find and complete tenant checks, produce inventories, and collect your rental income. They will also complete regular checks on your investment while tenanted and feedback to you any actions required. So you really do not have to do everything yourself. In–fact you should view your investment property as a business – your retirement business. And just as a business utilises the skills and working capacity of employees you need to do the same to maximise the smooth running and return on your investment.

Summary

In Section One of this book we spent considerable time going through the various elements which have colluded to produce a toxic retirement situation for millions.

Now in Section Two, we've seen how Property investment should form part of your pension planning, as it counteracts many of the factors negatively impacting your existing pension prospects. However such statements I believe are easy to write, only 'proof and facts' will strengthen the message and make it more compelling and dynamic.

Section Three of this book will reintroduce David, our 50 year old, who has just realised he has 16 years to address his huge pension shortfall. We will go on a journey with David to prove that the right type of property investment really can act as his Retirement Rescue Plan.

Section
Three

Property Investment as a Pension –
the Proof

10. David – His Shortfall

Current Situation

As we know David is going to be 50 years old this year and he is an IT Project Manager. Since age 35 years he has been contributing to his Company Pension Scheme.

His contributions equate to 4% of his salary and his employer has been contributing 5%. Under his Company's Pension Scheme the 'Total Expense Ratio' quoted for his pension fund is 1.5% pa.

As a Basic Rate Tax Payer David has benefited over the last 15 years from 20% tax relief on his pension contributions.

However having just received his Annual Pension Statement he sees his fund value currently stands at only £58,725. And it's projected, if he carries on saving at his current level and the Fund grows at 5% pa, to be worth £203,120 when he comes to retirement age.

This is lower than previous projections, so David is naturally rather apprehensive and decides perhaps now is the time to review how his pension plans are progressing.

He is only looking to insure his own life in retirement, but he does want his pension income to increase by 3% per annum, so he has a chance of keeping in–line with inflation. He has watched how his parents have struggled and moaned as it has got harder and harder for them to make ends meet as each year passes, and he is concerned that eventually he will have to help support them. This has added to his desire to ensure his pension pays out for a minimum term of 5 years, so should he pass away early in his retirement his whole pension pot, which he has worked so hard to save, is not lost.

David searches the Internet and discovers the best rate for a 'Single life, 3% escalation, 5yr guaranteed', Annuity is 4.073%. So based on his projected pension pot of £203,120 David calculates his retirement income from his 31 years of contributions to his Company Pension will only be an income of:

£203,120 x 4.073% = **£8,273 pa**

David is horrified and completely overwhelmed as he has already calculated he needs an income of £24,500pa to provide him with the retirement he had envisaged. Even allowing for the State Pension he still needs his Company Pension to deliver an income of £17,012 pa. Which of course by the time he comes to retire in 16 years, based on inflation at 2.94% pa, will need to be equal to £26,273 to retain the same purchasing power. This means David is currently projecting a pension shortfall of £18,000.

Figure 1 helps illustrates the size of this Pension Shortfall.

Figure 1

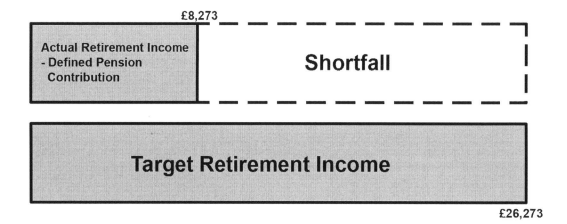

Figure 2 is a reminder of David's Pension as it currently stands.

Figure 2

David's Pension Summary	
Assumptions	
Average inflation throughout working life is	2.94%
David's salary has risen in line with inflation	
David's Pension contributions have been	4%
David's Employer's contributions have been	5%
David's pension fund annual interest earned	5%
Fund Management Fees (TER) pa	1.50%
Annuity Rate for Single Life, 3% escalation 5 Yr guarantee	4.073%

David is now 50	
His current salary is	£42,780
His current pension fund is valued at	£58,725
David's desired retirement income at today's prices	£24,500
The current State Pension at £144 per week is	£7,488
Therefore, income to be generated by pension is	£17,012

When David is Age 65	
His salary will be	£66,070
His pension fund will be worth	£203,120
This will buy an annuity of	£8,273
With inflation, income to be generated by pension will be	£26,273

David's Retirement Income at Age 65	
Retirement Income to be generated by pension	£26,273
Less Annuity Income	£8,273
David's Pension Shortfall	**£18,000**

11. David – Options for the Future

Now that David fully understands the size of his pension shortfall he realises he needs to take action, and fast. Unfortunately, procrastination will not resolve his personal pension crisis, neither will hoping it will all sort itself out.

David realizes he has two choices:

1. Put more money into his existing pension to make up the shortfall or,
2. Maintain his 4% contributions to his company pension but invest in an alternative solution to make up the shortfall.

Option 1 – How much more will David need to invest in his Pension to make–up the shortfall?

David works out that to meet his £18,000 pension shortfall on an annuity rate of 4.073% he would require an additional pension fund of £441,933, which would take his total pension pot to £645,053.

His monthly contributions of 4% of his salary over the last 15 years have only built him a pot worth £203,120 so he now has only 16 years remaining before retirement. To make up the additional money is a tall order as the cost of the additional contributions will need to come from David's salary alone, since his employer will not be increasing the company's 5% contribution.

David calculates that if he is to fill his pension shortfall by increasing his contributions then he will have to start paying £1,242 from his pay–packet each month. This means increasing his monthly contributions from 4% to a massive 43.5%, and maintaining this painfully high figure for the remaining 16 years he is planning to work. This additional investment is going to cost him £271,479 on top of the existing £27,464 he has already committed to his pension.

The table over the page, is a summary of David's pension requirements to make up his shortfall:

Figure 11

David's Pension Requirements to Make Up Shortfall	
When David is Age 65	
His Salary will be	£66,070
His pension pot will be worth	£203,120
This will buy an annuity of (rate = 4.073%)	£8,273
But the income David requires will have grown with inflation to	£26,273
His Pension Shortfall will be	**£18,000**
To meet this shortfall will require an additional Pension Pot of	£441,933

Which will require an increase in contributions from Age 50 to Age 65	
Contributions will now need to be increased to	43.50%

The Value of David's Contributions	
David's contributions from 50 to 65 at 4% will total	£27,464
David's contributions from 50 to 65 at 43.54% will total	£298,943
Total Extra Investment David will need to make	**£271,479**

Unsurprisingly, David feels tremendous pressure. He has £21,000 of other savings but knows this will not be enough to support him in his old age. However, maintaining such a high percentage of his income as a monthly contribution for 16 years is just untenable. Also even if he were to support this higher level of contribution he knows there are no guarantees that his pension shortfall will be filled 100%.

What if the Stock Market has a further tough time just before he is he due to retire or annuity rates drop further?

David does however believe that it is important to have a pension and he wishes to maintain his current level of contributions, not least because it gives him the opportunity to leverage both his employer for their 5% contributions but also because he can benefit from tax relief. But now he understands the reality of the situation he realises he can't afford to have all his eggs in one basket and rely on his pension to form 100% of his retirement planning.

David desperately needs to add some certainty to his pension planning and believes he needs to diversify to spread his risk, but he knows he doesn't have the luxury of time on his side, and doesn't want to make the wrong decision.

To help David to review the different options open to him to fill his 'pension shortfall' I have designed the simple risk chart shown below.

Risk Level 1: White
- Represents the lowest risk because it provides the greatest certainty of the desired outcome

Risk Level 10: Black
- Represents the highest risk because it has the lowest certainty of achieving the desired outcome.

Figure 12

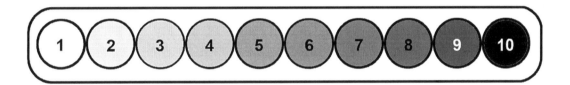

The general rule of investing is the greater the risk taken, the greater the capacity to deliver higher rewards. However, you must go into higher risk investments with your eyes open and you need to be able to sustain a loss, or lower growth than projected, as the probability of this happening is of course far greater.

So as David currently feels his fingers have already been burnt he wants to ensure the solution he now follows moves him down the risk scale to a level where he feels comfortable.

Everyone's level of comfort will be different based on their own personal circumstances, and you will need to determine your own 'risk level'.

I will help you with this in Chapter 30, 'Your 15 Step Retirement Rescue Plan '.

12. Risk Profile of a Defined Contribution Pension Fund

Through no fault of his own, David's pension and many others' have moved from mid risk to high risk and I would currently award a Defined Contribution Pension a risk score of "8", based on the key facts we have already discussed.

Figure 13

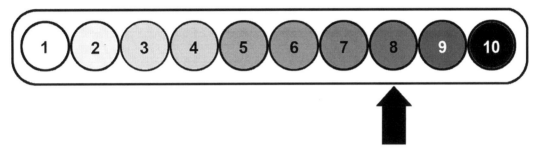

In particular:

    i.   Most people have no comprehension about the amount of money they need to pay into a pension fund each month, to achieve their desired outcome. "Starting late" means the effect of compound growth is limited.

    ii.   Pension fund performance has been poor over the last decade. Even the rally in the Stock Market of late can't make up for the lost years.

    iii.   Those who have been saving have been misled with unrealistic projections based on 5%, 7% and 9% compounded. And these overstated projections will continue on websites and in documentation until April 2014, when all will be amended to 2%, 5% and 8% growth rates. How can investors make the right decisions if the facts are incorrect?

    iv.   Annuity rates have fallen dramatically and few predict that they will rise significantly in the near future.

    v.   As those saving move closer to retirement, pension funds tend to follow a principle called 'Life styling', whereby they move the saved funds into Bonds as these are deemed less volatile than Equities. However, with all the money that has been pumped into Bonds in recent months an artificial 'Bond Bubble' has been created, and now people are leaving the Bond market in droves. Although lower Bond prices will increase the yields, this could mean that saved pension fund values are slashed right at the time they need to be protected.

Taking our illustration of David we have shown the extent to which Defined Contribution Pensions have shifted dramatically to the right on the risk scale.

Our focus therefore in the remaining Chapters of this book is to ascertain whether Property investment can provide the 'life support' required for retirement, while offering a greater probability of certainty.

13. Can Property Outperform a Pension?

Property investment is not a main stay solution offered in the Press, and where Buy To Let is discussed it is often in negative terms. So it would be natural for you to wonder how it can offer a better solution to your retirement plans than your pension. After–all wouldn't it be even riskier?

We have already looked at it from a diversification point of view but if we now look at each of the elements of Property investment which can cause anxiety and expense and address them one by one, then you will be able to understand how Property investment fits healthily within a pension plan. Each will be included in a modelling exercise to analyse financially the performance of Property v a Pension in filling David's pension shortfall.

As we already know the additional money that David will have to place in his pension to potentially fill his income void is £271,479 – the question is:

'Can we use property to achieve the same effect but for less cost than this?'

So let's begin

Financing Your Investment

Purchasing an investment property will require money, however you don't need the full amount of money, as we have already discussed there is power in leveraging a Mortgage. Mortgages allow you to utilise other people's money to build your pension, so you will actually only require a 25% deposit. (There were a few Buy To Let Mortgages available at 80% Loan to Value, but for the purposes of our calculations we will be working on a 75% Loan to Value ratio, as it provides a more secure investment).

In fact when looking to finance a deposit the cheapest way is from your cash savings, but as this is not always feasible remortgaging equity from your home can also be a highly effective solution.

To add strength to the modelling calculations I have chosen to work from a "worst case" scenario and as a result the deposit and associated investment costs will all come from a re–mortgage of David's own home.

I want to take this opportunity to fundamentally prove you can make the equity within your home "work effectively for you" and build your pension.

In the calculations therefore the rental income from each investment property will look to support two mortgages:

i.   The Buy to Let Mortgage – Interest Only or Repayment
ii.   The Residential Offset Re–mortgage – Repayment basis only.

Mortgage rates are currently highly competitive. However you need to remember interest rates are fluid, so please see over the page a selection of interest rates from Sept 2013 for both Offset Residential and Buy To Let Mortgages.

It is important to make reference to why I have selected an Offset Remortgage on your home. This is simply due to the fact it will be impossible to purchase your complete property portfolio simultaneously. An offset mortgage provides you the benefits of being able to remortgage the full money you require in one go and then offset it against your remortgage value, only paying for it as and when you spend it. i.e. your total borrowing is £100,000, but you only need £20,000 for purchase of the first property. When you complete on the Sale you will start paying for borrowing the £20,000, the remaining £80,000 continues to sit in your offset bank account until required.

The mortgage product you are able to secure will depend on several variables, so my advice would be to speak to your Independent Mortgage Broker. Also remember your home is at risk if you do not keep up repayments on a mortgage or other loan secured on it, so your Mortgage Broker will help you ascertain the level of funds you will be able to afford to release.

Figure 14

Examples of Buy To Let Mortgage Rates (Purchase – First Time Landlords)			
BTL Term	**Current Interest Rate @ 75% LTV**	**Modelling Interest Rate**	**Contingency built into Modelling Calculations**
BTL – 2 Year Fixed	2.99%	6%	3.01%
BTL – 3 Year Fixed	3.99%	6%	2.01%
BTL – 5 Year Fixed	4.69%	6%	1.31%

Examples of Residential Offset Mortgage Rates (Remortgage)			
Term	**Current Interest Rate @ 75% LTV**	**Modelling Interest Rate**	**Contingency built into Modelling Calculations**
Resid – 2 Year Fixed	2.29%	6%	3.71%
Resid – 3 Year Fixed	2.64%	6%	3.36%
Resid – 5 Year Fixed	3.29%	6%	2.71%

In the modelling calculations I have chosen to work with an interest rate of 6%, which you can see from Figure 14 above provides a considerable contingency, when compared with current rates.

Why have I chosen 6%?

I have chosen 6% as it represents a commonly accepted long–term run rate and offers some stress–testing, however if you feel I have been over cautious with the contingency levels, you can feel comfortable the savings we will share are under–estimated, rather than exaggerated.

Both mortgages have also been calculated on an aggressive 16 year term, as we know David only has this length of time to address his pension shortfall. Again, if you have more years available before you retire the benefits offered by property can be even further enhanced.

So Which type of Mortgage is the Best Fit?

Traditionally, Buy To Let investors are renowned for purchasing investment property on an "Interest Only" basis. However, as we are looking for a retirement solution which offers both stability and certainty we will be reviewing the financial performance from both an Interest Only and Repayment Mortgage viewpoint. I feel it's important to do this as the two investment strategies are very different.

The key advantages and disadvantages of each mortgage type in relation to pension provision are shown below.

Advantages of a Repayment Mortgage

i. With a Repayment Mortgage you repay the capital along with the interest over the term of the mortgage. This means from a retirement viewpoint you have 100% certainty at the end of the term (assuming all payments have been made) you will own the property out right. The ideal scenario for your pension.

ii. Initially the repayment of capital seems slow with most of the money being attributed to interest, however on a 16 year mortgage around year seven there is a tipping point where the monthly Mortgage payments switch to aggressively reducing the capital element. Figure 15 over the page illustrates this based on a £45k mortgage, but the principle is the same for any mortgage value.

Figure 15

Repayment Mortgage Example

Purchase Price	£60,000
Mortgage @ 75% LTV	£45,000
Interest Rate	6.00%

Year	Capital Outstanding at Start of Each Year	Capital Repaid	Interest Paid	Monthly Payment
1	£45,000	£1,729	£2,653	£365.15
2	£43,271	£1,835	£2,547	£365.15
3	£41,436	£1,949	£2,433	£365.15
4	£39,487	£2,069	£2,313	£365.15
5	£37,418	£2,196	£2,186	£365.15
6	£35,222	£2,332	£2,050	£365.15
7	£32,890	£2,476	£1,906	£365.15
8	£30,414	£2,628	£1,754	£365.15
9	£27,786	£2,791	£1,591	£365.15
10	£24,995	£2,962	£1,420	£365.15
11	£22,033	£3,146	£1,236	£365.15
12	£18,887	£3,339	£1,043	£365.15
13	£15,548	£3,545	£837	£365.15
14	£12,003	£3,764	£618	£365.15
15	£8,239	£3,996	£386	£365.15
16	£4,243	£4,243	£139	£365.15
		£45,000	£25,112	

iii. As the debt falls your exposure to any increase in interest rates also reduces. At the end of year seven the outstanding debt would be £30,414 (i.e. start of year eight), which represents a 33% reduction on the original debt. This means if you wished to remortgage to benefit from new interest rates you would require a lower Loan to Value (LTV) mortgage.

iv. In addition, to point iii above, the silent benefit of inflationary erosion on the real value of the debt and the potential for house prices to rise, means your Loan to Value ratio will significantly strengthen all the time. This again will open up more competitive interest rates and provide you with an overall improving financial position, which is favourable in retirement.

Figure 16

Capital Outstanding at Start of Each Year

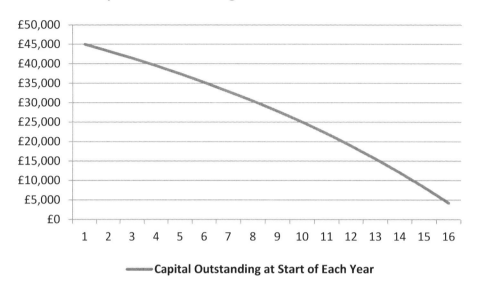

━━━━Capital Outstanding at Start of Each Year

v. You can even increase your certainty by fixing your interest rates for a longer term.

vi. A further advantage of a Repayment Mortgage is that if you overpay the monthly payment, even by a relatively small amount, you can dramatically shorten the mortgage term.

In our example if we were to overpay our mortgage payment by 10% (i.e. an extra £36.50 per month) then we would reduce the mortgage term by a full 2 years and 4 months, saving £4,006 of interest payment (calculated using the Overpayment Calculator on www.moneysavingexpert.com)

This flexibility offered by the Repayment Mortgage is a fundamental advantage and as long as you stay within the terms and conditions of your mortgage you will not be subject to any Early Redemption Charges.

Disadvantages of a Repayment Mortgage

As you would expect, counterbalancing the advantages there are a few disadvantages, these are:

i.   During the term of the mortgage the monthly payments will be considerably higher than an Interest Only Mortgage.

ii.   By paying off your mortgage early you will not benefit from the maximum inflationary erosion of the 'real value' of your mortgage.

iii. Paying off your mortgage is not quite as tax efficient as an Interest Only Mortgage, as the interest element of your mortgage payment which can be offset against tax is reducing month on month.

In summary, however, from a retirement income viewpoint a Repayment Mortgage over 16 years offers a high degree of certainty and so on my risk profile scores a Level 3.

Figure 17

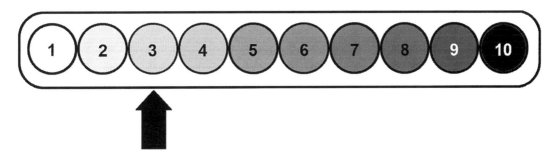

So how do Interest Only Buy To Let Mortgages compare?

Advantages of Interest Only Mortgages

i.   During the term of the mortgage you will achieve higher returns (cash flow) since you are only paying the interest element on the borrowed money.

ii.   You can benefit from the full erosional power of inflation on the 'real value' of your mortgage debt. The debt will remain constant (ie at £45,000) but the value of the debt will fall with inflation overtime. For example at the end of a 16 year term with inflation at 2.94% per annum the original debt of £45k will be equivalent to only £28k in today's money. So inflation will have literally eroded 38% of the 'value' of the debt.

iii. As the full debt figure is outstanding for the term of the mortgage, the interest payment remains high, and this full payment can be offset against Tax.

Disadvantages of Interest Only Mortgages

i. The major disadvantage is that at the end of the mortgage term, the full debt will be outstanding and you still need to pay it back to the bank.

At this stage you will have one of three choices:

a. repay the debt from savings or shares etc.
b. sell the property to repay the debt.
c. remortgage the property

a) Utilising this choice would only be possible if you know you have access to additional money at the required time.

b) Will mean you cease to have the asset which is going to produce your monthly retirement income. If there is spare money from the sale (after you have paid all associated costs including Capital Gains Tax) you could invest this for an income, but again you will be faced with the challenge of where to invest to get the best return. Selling the property can also leave you at the mercy of the housing market at that time. After all there is no guarantee in 16 years the house value will be exactly where you need it to be and a time forced sale may necessitate a reduced price.

c) This option will only be available if in 16 years' time the lenders allow you to borrow into your retirement. Unfortunately, no one can predict lender criteria that far into the future, so again you run the risk of having to sell if you can't clear the debt via any other route. And even if you were able to remortgage having to pay a mortgage would significantly reduce your monthly income in retirement.

ii. The second major disadvantage of Interest Only Mortgages is that they leave you more exposed to interest rate fluctuations. This is great news when rates are going down, but can easily eat into cash flow when rates rise (at the moment rates are so very low that any future movement will almost certainly be up).

iii. As the debt remains constant, if you wish to remortgage you are completely reliant on the house value to determine the loan to value ratio. In a stagnant or falling market this may mean you are unable to get access to the more competitive interest rates i.e. at 60% LTV.

iv.   You will pay more interest over the term of the mortgage. In the table over the page you can see the monthly payments are lower than for a Repayment Mortgage, but the total interest paid over the 16 years is significantly higher at just over £43,000. In Figure 15 you will notice it was only just over £25,000 (ie 42% lower). And having paid more interest overall, the £45,000 of debt is still outstanding as illustrated by the line on the graph remaining level.

Figure 18

Interest Only Mortgage Example	

Purchase Price	£60,000
Mortgage @ 75% LTV	£45,000
Interest Rate	6.00%

Year	Capital Outstanding at Start of Each Year	Capital Repaid	Interest Paid	Monthly Payment
1	£45,000	£0	£2,700	£225.00
2	£45,000	£0	£2,700	£225.00
3	£45,000	£0	£2,700	£225.00
4	£45,000	£0	£2,700	£225.00
5	£45,000	£0	£2,700	£225.00
6	£45,000	£0	£2,700	£225.00
7	£45,000	£0	£2,700	£225.00
8	£45,000	£0	£2,700	£225.00
9	£45,000	£0	£2,700	£225.00
10	£45,000	£0	£2,700	£225.00
11	£45,000	£0	£2,700	£225.00
12	£45,000	£0	£2,700	£225.00
13	£45,000	£0	£2,700	£225.00
14	£45,000	£0	£2,700	£225.00
15	£45,000	£0	£2,700	£225.00
16	£45,000	£0	£2,700	£225.00
		£0	£43,200	

Figure 19

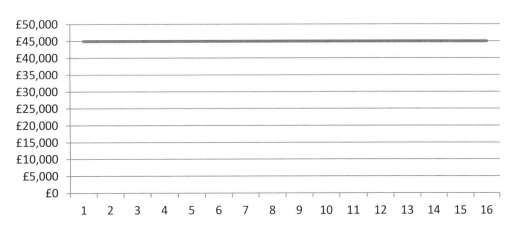

Capital Outstanding at Start of Each Year

━━━Capital Outstanding at Start of Each Year

Taking this all into consideration for retirement risk purposes I have placed Interest Only Mortgages at Level 7.

Figure 20

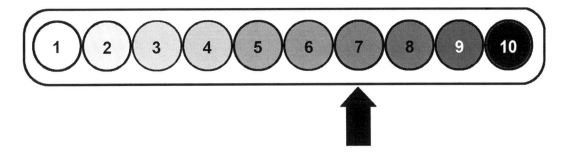

Understanding the fundamental differences between an Interest Only Mortgage and a Repayment Mortgage when planning for retirement is essential, and an area which is often skimmed over in the interests of driving for cash–flow and income tax efficiencies (we will cover this in more detail later on in this Chapter).

However, I believe it is of paramount importance when establishing your own personal strategy. So the graphic below provides a summary of the key factors which differentiate the two types of mortgage.

Figure 21

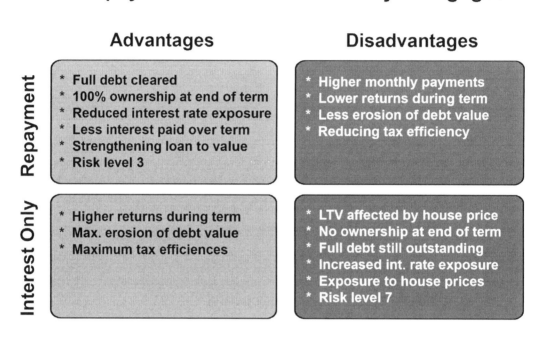

Repayment versus Interest Only Mortgages

Advantages

Repayment
* Full debt cleared
* 100% ownership at end of term
* Reduced interest rate exposure
* Less interest paid over term
* Strengthening loan to value
* Risk level 3

Interest Only
* Higher returns during term
* Max. erosion of debt value
* Maximum tax efficiences

Disadvantages

* Higher monthly payments
* Lower returns during term
* Less erosion of debt value
* Reducing tax efficiency

* LTV affected by house price
* No ownership at end of term
* Full debt still outstanding
* Increased int. rate exposure
* Exposure to house prices
* Risk level 7

Purchasing Costs – Associated with your Investment

These costs are often overlooked, but they form an essential element when comparing the performance of Property investment with a pension.

Consequently, in the financial modelling I have allowed for the following property costs:

- 25% deposit
- Valuation and Solicitor's fees
- Refurbishment costs incl. Marketing Costs (of between £7,500 – £9,000 dependent on House Value)
- Sourcing "Hands–Free" Fees / Education

Your Deposit

We have already discussed that the cheapest way to raise your deposit is from your savings. However, in the financial model I have again assumed the 'worse case' financial situation, where all the above purchase costs, including your deposit, are raised as a remortgage against your main residence. This remortgage must 'ALWAYS' be on a Repayment basis to ensure you do not take debt on your home into retirement. To this end, the modelling has been based on a 16 year Repayment Mortgage at 6% interest rate.

Valuation and Solicitor's Fees

In completing our comparisons against a pension I have included £2,000 per purchase to cover Valuation and Solicitor's Fees, for both the Remortgage and the Buy To Let purchase. Realistically you will probably raise the investment capital from your home only once so there would only be one set of Valuation and Solicitor's fees on this property. However, for simplicity I have kept the costs the same on each transaction.

Refurbishment Costs

Adding value to your investment by cosmetic refurbishment is a very sensible and popular investment strategy. The skill comes in:

- accurately costing out the money required for the refurbishment (and checking it still makes the purchase a good deal)
- sticking to your budget

This refurbishment will need to come from your savings or capital raised from the remortgage of your home, as it cannot be included in the BTL Mortgage.

Under–estimating refurbishment costs is a common error made by novice investors. Tasks which look minor can soon add up and eat into the equity of the property. The more detailed and thorough you can be in the early stages of viewing a property the better it is as you can minimise any nasty surprises.

When purchasing property for ourselves and my clients I arrange to view with my builder to have the benefit of his expertise and to ensure that he fully understands and agrees with the amount and scope of the work that needs to be done. We walk from room to room carefully noting down everything that requires attention and what level of work is deemed necessary so that he can quote against my specific requirements.

Of the 34 houses I've purchased and refurbished (at the time of writing), a high proportion have been repossessions. This has meant that each one has been truly individual with regard to the amount of work necessary to get it ready for tenants so a personal site visit has been essential. In any property the obvious areas for refurbishment are the kitchen and bathroom but it is important not to overlook other parts, so go systematically throughout the house viewing each room from ceiling to floor.

You will be looking to see what needs replacing, repairing or renovating and, hopefully, what is quite acceptable and can be retained. Use your eyes, and your nose, to detect any problems that could be expensive to overcome but are not immediately obvious. Buying an investment property is a big commitment and you can't afford to get it wrong so, if in doubt, seek professional advice.

Be nosy, look into cupboards, under the stairs and in the loft. If possible, make a note of the manufacturer and style of the central heating boiler so you can check it on the internet later. Is it an obsolete model and likely to need imminent replacement? Is it covered by any Government boiler replacement schemes?

When you have noted, as much as possible about the property without actually living there, go outside and have a thorough look at the exterior. Again study every aspect and take note of any danger signs such as broken roof tiles, damp patches on the walls, crumbling rendering or pointing, rotten woodwork, damp proof course covered by soil, broken paving/concrete, damaged fencing, etc., and agree with your builder what repairs are necessary and are to be included in his quotation.

Until you have established a team that you are comfortable with, it is advisable to get more than one quote for the required work. In addition you must allow for the Electrical Certificate and Gas Certificate that the law demands, plus the checks and any remedial work necessary to bring your property up to the required standard for these certificates.

The important thing to remember is that your property portfolio is a business, so you do not need to install the latest designer kitchen or exotic decorations. However, you do have a duty of care to your tenants so safe, simple, practical and robust is the order of the day with light, neutral colours to appeal to a wide range of tastes. Even when you have established your specification and received quotations, I would recommend a 15% – 20% contingency to allow for any items that have been overlooked or plans that need to be reworked due to unforeseen circumstances.

In our modelling calculations I have worked with realistic refurbishments figures based on my own experience and have increased the budget based on the purchase price of the house. More expensive houses are generally larger, so there is more to refurbish, or they are in areas where labour costs are higher.

The figures I have included are shown below.

Figure 22

Purchase Price	Refurbishment Cost Included in Modelling
£50,000 – £65,000	£7,500
£75,000 – £100,000	£8,000
£124,500	£9,000

Sourcing Costs – Your Investment Property

You have two choices:

    i.   Source the property yourself
    ii.   Work with a company who will find the property for you

Which route is right for you will depend on how you view the relationship between time and money.

Certainly if you are employed (like David) or self–employed there can seem to be few hours in the day and time is a very precious commodity. Unfortunately, an all too quickly approaching retirement will heighten that feeling, as you certainly don't have the luxury of letting time just pass you by without taking positive action.

So if you are already overstretched and the thought of adding more workload fills you with dread and will stop you from addressing your pension shortfall, the best thing you can do is to be honest with yourself, and hire someone else to help you.

There are a range of different offerings in this area:

- **Sourcer** – 'Do what it says on the tin' i.e. they simply source the property. At that point their responsibility stops so the investor needs to arrange the refurbishment, identify and co–ordinate with the Letting Agent etc.

- **Hands–Free / Armchair Investors** – these companies source the property on a one by one basis, and manage the refurbishment on behalf of the investor. They then liaise with Letting Agents who manage the property on behalf of the investor. Some companies offer their own in–house Letting Agent, while others utilise the expertise of independent agents.

- **Portfolio Builders** – require a large upfront financial commitment to build a portfolio of houses within a given time frame. This approach incorporates the financial model we will discuss in Chapter 25, and due diligence is essential to ensure the results are as desired.

In my calculations I have allowed for the average cost of the full Hands–Free investing approach. This is the system I work with my clients in Alton Property Partners and it ensures myself and my team take all the strain of the workload without the requirement for my clients to commit to large sums of money upfront. We source the houses on a 1 by 1 basis, document and cost out the refurbishment, complete the financial review and work with the Estate Agent. We of course also have access to an Independent Mortgage Broker, via Alton Mortgages Ltd to handle the mortgage finance.

Then once the offer has been accepted, we coordinate the refurbishment work and liaise with the Letting Agent regarding the marketing of the property. The graphic below provides an overview of the stages of this service.

Figure 23

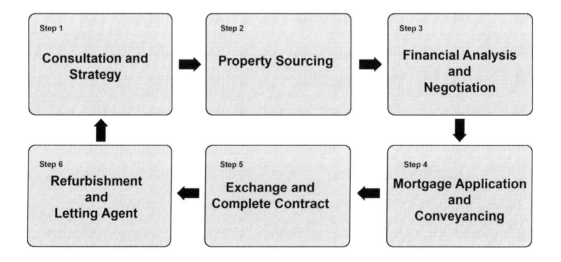

Advantages of a Hands–Free Service

Hands–free investment services are very much designed for the busy professional and they also offer the advantage of being able to invest in locations where you don't actually live. They give you the opportunity to leverage the skill of seasoned professionals to build your pension, but on a 1 by 1 basis so you are keeping full control.

In my calculations I have allowed for an average Hands Free fee of £5,000 for each property. You may find that some companies, like Alton Property Partners, offer a sliding scale of costs based on the number of houses you commit to purchasing, but for simplicity I have kept it at a constant £5,000.

Education

Alternatively, if you have time on your hands to complete the investing yourself, and relish the challenge you can utilise the £5,000 to educate yourself. There are a multitude of businesses which offer Property Educational Programmes, from Mentoring One to One (like Alton Property Mentoring), to big classroom environments.

You can choose the fit that is right for you based on your preferred learning style. One thing is for sure if you are planning to fill your pension shortfall by investing yourself I would thoroughly recommend you don't cut corners, and you take the time to educate yourself.

I will provide you with some guidance on how to choose the right partner to work with in Chapter 28, 'Investing Yourself or Choosing a Hands–Free Property Partner'.

Summary of Purchasing Costs

From a modelling point of view let me summarise, the figures I have used. They are:

i.   A remortgage on your own home based on a Repayment Mortgage with a 16 year term, at 6% interest rate. This money will cover

  - 25% deposit for the Buy to Let purchase
  - Solicitor's and Valuation fees of £2,000
  - Refurbishment costs ranging from the £7500 – £9,000 (incl. Marketing Costs)
  - Hands–Free property investment Fee / Property Education costs of £5000

ii.	A Buy to Let Mortgage based on a 75% Loan to Value basis. The modelling has compared the pension performance to property based on both a Repayment and Interest Only basis at 6% interest rate

Ongoing costs

But don't houses cost money to run? And what if you have voids and rogue tenants?

Firstly, and most importantly property investment needs to be viewed as a business so just like a business there are "operating costs" to consider. To provide a true comparison to a pension I have taken the following costs into consideration:

- Letting Agent
- Voids
- Insurance
- Maintenance
- Legal Obligations

Letting Agent

Unfortunately you are not getting any younger. However, just because you are an investor does not mean you need to be burdened with the day to day management of your properties. You need an employee in your business and that employee is your Letting Agent.

Your Letting Agent will be responsible for running the business "day–to–day" for you, so working with a reliable Letting Agent is fundamental to minimise the risks and concerns that are often quoted by 'would be investors' such as:

- *"but what if I get voids? I don't have time to show new tenants around"*
- *"what if the toilet breaks in the night I don't want to have to sort that out"*
- *"what are my legal obligations as a landlord"*

I would recommend you work with your Letting Agent on a fully managed service basis, as this means they will not only advertise and find the tenants for you but also complete the necessary credit checks / references, look after your tenants and importantly chase the rent for you.

They will also conduct regular reviews of your property to check your investment. Don't be tempted to cut corners and manage the properties yourself to save money, as in the long run this can be both time consuming and a burden. I would recommend your Letting Agent is an active member of a Trade Body like The Association of Residential Letting Agents (ARLA).

In terms of our pension v property calculations I have allowed for 10% letting fees plus VAT.

A Word of Warning – if you are unhappy with your Letting Agent, change them. However, remember it is your business and they are your employee so just as a traditional business owner would not leave an employee in charge indefinitely and expect the business to perform at its ultimate best, neither should you. Working with a Letting Agent removes the workload from you, but it would be short–sighted to abdicate complete responsibility for your houses. After–all it's your retirement income.

Voids – what if I get voids? Or tenants don't pay?

Fact – with rental property you will always get void periods, they cannot be completely avoided. Your focus should be on minimising the length and frequency of the episode. Here are some simple rules you can follow to reduce your risk of extended void periods:

(a) It is imperative you complete due diligence and purchase in an area where there is high rental demand to feed your type of property.

(b) Keep the maintenance up–to–date, as a general rule *"happy tenants pay and don't move out"*.

(c) Ensure your Letting Agent carries out all the necessary checks on your prospective tenants. These include credit checks, employee references and previous landlord references. Do not cut corners at this stage.

(d) I would recommend that you always take a deposit. If however the prospective tenant says they can't afford one then it is your choice whether you accept them or not as a tenant. If you do, I would recommend you look for a Home Owner Guarantor, ideally their parent. It is not as satisfactory as having a deposit but it adds a degree of certainty.

Non–paying tenants can indeed be stressful but there are ways of minimising this stress as you remove non–paying tenants from you properties.

Currently, if tenants on Housing Benefit are more than eight weeks late with their rent you can apply to the Council for the Benefit to be paid directly to your Letting Agent. However, Universal Credit originally due to be launched nationally in Quarter 3, 2013 (the national launch date is predicted to have slipped) will involve changes to the way Housing Benefit is paid.

At present full details are not available but the Government has confirmed that the top priority is to ensure that Housing Benefit still reaches the landlord. As such, they have built in a system to ensure that direct payment can again be achieved in the event of late payments. We are awaiting the full details.

You can also join a Rent Guarantee Scheme. Such schemes will cover the costs of any court cases relating to evictions and will ensure any rent due is received so you are not financially impacted. From a retirement viewpoint these schemes offer an additional layer of certainty to your pension income.

I would recommend you take time to understand the procedure for obtaining payment of rent arrears and evicting a tenant. Understand Sections 8 and 21 of the Housing Act 1988 and how to use them. Your Letting Agent and Solicitor will act on your behalf if you ever have to follow these procedures, but it is your responsibility to know when you can evoke them. After–all having the ability to maintain control of your investment is one of its major advantages, so a lack of knowledge or naivety on your behalf, can cost you financially.

If you look on the Internet there is a lot of data on this subject, below are just two links which you might find useful:

www.gov.uk/private–renting–evictions/rules–your–landlord–must–follow

www.landlordaction.co.uk/site.php/tenant/legal/residential_eviction_procedure

Based on our own portfolio, our average void period between tenant changes is circa two weeks, and we have found renting to families, rather than young professionals, adds a further layer of stability as they want to get their children settled and into the local schools etc. This means you would be highly unfortunate to experience a change of tenants at the end of each six–month Assured Short Hold tenancy (AST) agreement.

To allow for the reality of tenant movements however, I have based the occupancy level in my calculations on the average UK tenancy of 20 months and the average voids of three to four weeks. On this basis the occupancy rate is 95% per year. I have adopted this figure as it will allow for you to have maybe three weeks of void a year on one house, but only one week on another.

Insurance – what insurance would I need?

If you have a Buy To Let Mortgage you will be legally obliged by the lender to have Buildings Insurance live from the day of Exchange. Buildings Insurance protects both yourself and the lender in the event of any fundamental structural issue and even includes the cost of a complete rebuild.

Contents Cover on the other hand covers you for all items which do not form part of the building itself. We rent our houses unfurnished and so the initial entry–level Contents Cover of £5,000, which covers carpets etc., is more than adequate. Even if you furnish your property, in most cases you will not need to increase the Contents cover massively, I recommend you discuss this with your Mortgage Broker who can also advise on appropriate insurance products.

In–fact Independent Mortgage Brokers, like Alton Mortgages Ltd, have access to superior specialist BTL insurance that you are unable to find on the High Street. For this reason I would always recommend you work with your Broker to get the best and most competitive cover. Note: Malicious Damage and Rent Guarantee Schemes can also be included within policies. Again for the purposes of my calculations I have focused on providing the greatest level of certainty, while reducing risks as far as possible, so I've included the following costs which were provided by my husband (a Mortgage Broker):

(a) Buildings Insurance to include malicious damage based on a 3 bedroom house, semi–detached and occupied by tenants on Housing Benefit. Cover is based on the purchase price of the property and increased by inflation at 2.94% each year.

(b) £5,000 of Contents Cover with Malicious damage and Rent Guarantee.

Maintenance

We have already discussed that property investment should be viewed as your own income generating business, so like any business there are inputs which are required to generate the outputs. Ongoing maintenance is one of those inputs and is an essential element to maintaining your retirement income stream. Scrimping on maintenance can be a false economy for the following reasons:

(a) Happy tenants are more likely to pay.

(b) You are legally required to provide a "safe" house under the Landlord and Tenant Act 1985,

(c) Happy tenants are not only more likely to look after your property but more likely to stay long term removing the need for you to spend money marketing to find new tenants and covering any associated void periods.

(d) Regular maintenance maintains the capital value of your property.

Remember you're investing for the long term and want to do everything to ensure your income stream is maintained. That being said you do not want tenants to abuse your good nature, so working with your Letting Agent to ensure the tenants understand their responsibility can be helpful.

However, you do need to be prepared to pay for repairs and maintenance relating to general wear and tear. Here is a list of some issues we've experienced recently across our portfolio:

- A leaking shower
- A blown down fence panel
- A broken front door lock
- A leak in the kitchen
- A loose handrail

If you've already anticipated wear and tear costs and allowed for them in your financials, then you can take action quickly and decisively without having to stress where the money is coming from. For this reason I recommend to all my investors and mentees that they retain a "maintenance contingency pot". This should be held separately and include some of your initial seed capital to give the pot a boost.

I would then recommend you set up an automatic transfer from your rental account each month, so that a proportion of your rental income is used to feed the pot. That way you will constantly replenish your maintenance fund (which can also cover Council Tax liabilities during empty periods) and you won't become accustomed to living off every penny of cash–flow, only to find you suffer when a bill comes in.

In my modelling calculations I have included an annual maintenance allowance of 1% of the purchase price i.e. £50,000 house equals £500 per annum, £100,000 house equals £1,000 per annum. This allowance has then been increased by 2.94% per annum to allow for inflation.

Legal obligations – what are they? How much will they cost me?

If you are a new landlord it can be daunting to know your legal obligations, so I would recommend you refer to the internet as there are a number of good websites covering this subject. www.landlords.org.uk the website of The National Landlord Association is a very good starting point and offers a wealth of information regarding landlord's responsibilities.

Under Section One1 of the Landlord and Tenant Act 1985 you have a statutory obligation to keep your property, including its services (i.e. gas, electricity and sanitation), its structure and its exterior, in good repair.

(a) **Gas Safety Checks** – As part of these legal responsibilities you are required to complete an annual Gas Certificate by a Gas Safe qualified engineer (Gas Safe replaced Corgi). The cost will vary nationally so I have allowed for £80, which should cover any regional variations. In my modelling calculations this cost has then been increased annually over the 16 year term by 2.94% each year, to reflect inflationary rises.

   Note: if you have a change of tenant during the year you are required to redo the Gas Certificate, irrespective of the fact that you still within the valid 12 month period.

(b) **Electrical Certificate / PAT Test** – Although Electrical Certificates are currently not a legal requirement, as a landlord you are required by law to protect the safety of your tenants and their pets. The Electrical Certificate, therefore, gives you peace of mind that the electrics in the house are safe.

   It's worth remembering, if you purchase directly from the homeowner they will not have completed these checks on their own property, so you may well find you need to do extra work to bring the electrics up to the current standard.

   Unlike the Gas Certificate, the Electrical Certificate only needs to be renewed every five years. In my calculations I have included £180 (inflation linked) to cover this cost.

   If you opt to include white goods in your rental properties (I don't) you will need to have these PAT tested by the Electrician annually.

(c) **Energy Performance Certificate** – These only need to be completed every 10 years and the initial certificate is covered by the Estate Agent as it requirement of the Sale. For the purpose of our calculations I have excluded this cost.

Summary of Ongoing Costs

The comprehensive list over the page summarises the ongoing costs allowed for in the modelling calculations:

- Letting Agent fee at 10% +VAT
- Buildings Insurance with malicious damage (inflation linked)
- £5,000 Contents Insurance with the malicious damage and rent guarantee (based on LHA tenants)– Inflation linked
- Annual Maintenance costs based on of 1% of purchase price (inflation linked)
- 95% occupancy
- Annual Gas Safety checks – inflation linked
- Electrical Certification (every 5 years) – inflation linked
- Inflation has been applied to all costs which will rise over time, at an average rate of 2.94% over the 16 year period. This will ensure the costs are a true reflection during the full mortgage term.

Rental Income

Having compiled probably the most comprehensive list of property investment related costs for the accuracy of my calculations I have compared these to Gross Rental Yields ranging between 6% and 11%.

Just as it was important to work with realistic expense figures, it was also important that I incorporated a realistic figure for the projected increase in rental values over the 16 year term. As such, the calculations are based on a 2.5% increase per annum. Why 2.5%?

Table 701, Local Authority Housing Average Weekly Rents by Region in UK, from the period 1998/99 – 2011/12 found at www.gov.uk shows that the average increase in rental values over this 14 year period has actually been 4.23% pa. Therefore, in selecting a growth rate of 2.5% p.a. for the calculations I have once again been deliberately conservative. If in reality rents rise more aggressively than 2.5% pa the financial results achieved through property investment will be even greater.

For your background understanding, Local Housing rents are based on private rents, but currently set at the 30 percentile. This means that in a given area Housing Benefit tenants can live in approximately 30% of the housing stock (as the rent is at the right price for them). Housing Benefit rents are reviewed monthly and will change as private rents change.

Tax

I am not a Tax Specialist or an Accountant, but to provide a true like for like comparison between a pension and property investment (whether on Interest Only or Repayment) I have also taken tax into consideration in the calculations.

Rental income will attract tax on any profit made after 'allowable expenses' have been deducted. In our calculations 'allowable expenses' cover the costs incurred for the day–to–day running of the properties and for wear and tear repairs necessary to maintain a lettable standard. You cannot claim tax relief on expenditure for any items considered to be an improvement, or cost of Sale items such as the Estate Agent fees.

So, for example, if a kitchen needed the units replaced due to wear and tear and the original kitchen had six units which you choose to replace with ten units, the cost of the six would be a 'revenue expense', so could be offset against your Rental Income. The additional four units would need to be a Capital Expense. Your accountant can help you with this. Suffice to say the more expenses you can allocate to allowable revenue expenses the better.

In our calculations to keep it simple, I have allowed for 85% of the refurbishment costs to be allowable revenue expenses. Although this will of course vary with each property.

To recap from earlier 'allowable revenue expenses' include:

- Letting Agent's fees
- Accountant's fees
- Buildings and Contents insurance
- Mortgage Interest
- Maintenance and repairs, BUT NOT improvements
- Utility bills – Gas, Water and Electricity (during the refurbishment period and any voids)
- Ground Rent, Service Charges (not applicable in our calculations)
- Council Tax (during the refurbishment and any void period)
- Services such as, cleaning or gardening
- Other direct costs of letting the property, like phone calls, stationery and advertising, travelling to and from property networking events, or going to view your properties

If you choose to furnish your properties you also have the choice to claim either a "wear and tear allowance" or a "renewals allowance". And of course there is the Energy Saving Allowance already mentioned.

Since one of the major benefits of a pension is its tax efficiencies, I would recommend you work with your Accountant to ensure you achieve the tax relief on absolutely everything you are entitled to on your property portfolio. In fact working with a knowledgeable property Accountant you will find that property can also be extremely tax efficient.

Then having accounted for all your Allowable Expenses, one of the **major advantages** of Property Investment is the ability to be able to offset these expenses and carry any losses forward indefinitely. Meaning you can have a £0 tax bill.

In my calculations I have allowed for the relevant mortgage interest (Interest Only or Repayment) to be offset over the 16 year term. Certainly in the later years of the Repayment Mortgage, as the focus swings to aggressively repaying the capital (see Figure 15 page 97 if you wish to remind yourself of the payment pattern) the interest element reduces so there is tax to be paid. This tax has been allowed for in our calculations based on 40%.

However, from a Repayment Mortgage viewpoint at the end of the mortgage term you are guaranteed to hold an unencumbered property. The Interest Only Mortgage option certainly saves income tax along the route, but this is traded for Capital Gains Tax if your strategy is to sell some houses to clear the debt on others. We will discuss this in detail later.

Summary of Costs Included in the Financial Modelling

At this stage, I think it would be worth recapping on all the expenses I have loaded into my calculations.

Figure 24 over the page, shows the complete list and I am sure you will agree this represents a truly comprehensive and fully loaded analysis.

If Property still outperforms a Pension on this basis you can be assured we are indeed looking at a Pension Shortfall solution which is financially robust.

Figure 24

Summary of Financial Modelling

Purchasing Costs	
Residential Offset Remortgage on a 16 Year Repayment Term @ 6% to cover:	
Deposit for BTL Purchase	25%
Refurbishment Costs Ranging from £7k – £9k	£7k – £9k
Valuation and Solicitors Fees of £2k	£2k
HandsFree Sourcing Cost / Education of £5k	£5k
BTL Mortgage on a 16 Year Term @ 6% to be based on	
Repayment Mortgage or	
Interest Only Mortgage	

Ongoing Costs	
Fully Managed Letting Agent Fee (based on 95% occupancy)	10% +VAT
Buildings Insurance with Malicious Damage (inflation linked)	£220 pa
Contents Insurance, with Rental Guarantee (inflation linked) based on	£255 pa
Annual Maintenance based on Purchase Price (inflation linked) at	1%
Annual Gas Safety Check (inflation linked)	£80
Electrical Certification (5 yearly – inflation linked)	£180
Tax on Rental Income (based on offsetting 85% of refurb costs as allowable expenses)	40%

Income	
Rental Income @ Gross Rental Yields of 6% – 11%, (based on 95% occupancy) increasing each year by	2.50%

14. The Ultimate Pension Solution?

The remaining chapters of this book detail the results of the modelling analysis, so we can determine whether David has another option open to him to fill his pension shortfall. An option which will not only cost him less, but hopefully, also pay him more in retirement.

Of course, one element that makes comparing Property investment to a pension particularly challenging is the different size of the units involved. A house is probably the largest capital outlay you're likely to make, whereas a pension can be saved pound by pound.

When completing the comparison between a pension and Property investment there are four different outcomes, which are illustrated in the graphic over the page.

The 'ultimate property solution' is represented by the top Right–Hand Corner.

This ultimate solution will allow you to achieve more retirement income to fill your pension shortfall, even though your personal contributions are less than those required for a pension.

Our focus now is on testing if this scenario really is possible. However, before we go on to do this it's worth just reminding ourselves of David's current situation, one last time:

David has paid into his company pension for the last 15 years, but due to underperformance on the growth and dramatically lower Annuity Rates has just realised that he has an £18,000 shortfall to the pension income he desires in retirement, namely £24,500.

Figure 25

Four Possible Property Outcomes

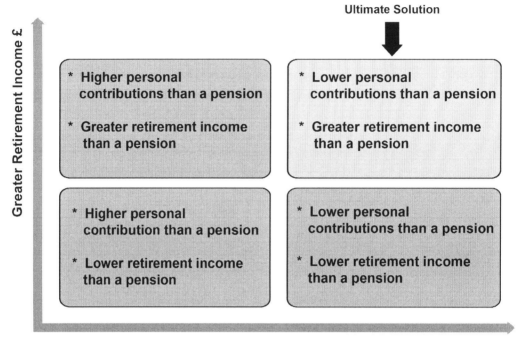

Ultimate Solution

Greater Retirement Income £ (vertical axis)

* Higher personal contributions than a pension

* Greater retirement income than a pension

* Lower personal contributions than a pension

* Greater retirement income than a pension

* Higher personal contribution than a pension

* Lower retirement income than a pension

* Lower personal contributions than a pension

* Lower retirement income than a pension

Lower Personal Contributions £

David is trying to assess whether there is an alternative solution to simply pumping more money into his pension to fill this gap, as he is nervous about putting 'more good money after bad'. He has every intention of remaining in his occupational pension scheme as this entitles him to tax relief plus his employer's contributions to further boost his pension savings. However, he has calculated that he would need to save an additional £271,479 to fill this gap over the next 16 years and this is a daunting figure, since it represents 43.5% of his income each month – a very tall order indeed.

David's shortfall calculations have been based on the following key facts:

- A Pension Growth rate of 5% compound per annum
- Lower Rate Tax Relief (David has just dipped into the Higher Rate band, but for simplicity we are keeping our calculations at the Lower Rate band)
- A Total Expense Ratio (ie fees and charges combined) on his Pension of 1.5%
- Inflation at 2.94% per annum
- An Annuity rate for a Single Life, 3% Escalating, 5 Yr Guarantee of 4.073%

Our Aim

Our aim is to understand through financial analysis whether Property Investment will deliver him the ultimate solution. Can he achieve higher retirement income from Property than a Pension? Can he meet or exceed his pension shortfall despite having made lower personal contributions?

Important: It is important to remember in both scenarios David has 16 years to turn his fortunes around, so it is imperative he increases his monthly financial commitment to his future. Our focus is on identifying which option costs less and yet gains greater certainty and control over his future and provides more income.

So if Property investment proves to be a viable option for David, can he buy any property or are there certain performance criteria he needs to satisfy to achieve his goal?

15. Is all Property the Same?

The simple answer to this question is "No". To achieve the desired outcome David needs to focus on achieving cash–flow, as this is the essential ingredient in the investing formula. Capital growth is a longer term bonus.

Those landlords who purchased Off Plan Properties in 2006 / 2007, or who remortgaged every pound of equity out of their properties, gearing themselves highly and forgetting the market is cyclical, are those who have felt the greatest pain during the latest house price correction. Their attraction to equity at the expense of cash–flow has cost them dearly.

Cash–flow is king, as it is cash flow that will give you a pension income.

So taking all the property costs into consideration, as detailed in Figure 24 is there a Gross Rental Yield which will deliver a cash–flow to out–perform a pension?

Gross Rental Yield is calculated as:

Annual Rent / Purchase Price x 100

e.g. Purchasing a house at £65,000 with a monthly rent of £500 (£6,000 pa) would deliver a Gross Rental Yield of 9.2%.

Although I would normally warn against being misled by the Gross Rental Yield, as it does not take into account any work required on the house to make it rentable, or any ongoing costs, we have allowed for all of these in our calculations. So in our case, using the Gross Rental yield to compare one property against another, forms a sound basis on which to make decisions.

So taking David's scenario into consideration and all the property costs we have covered in the previous chapters, what Gross Rental Yield does David need to ensure his properties out perform his pension option?

The figure overleaf shows the Gross Rental Yields that David needs to achieve to ensure his property investment provides him with a stronger financial solution than additional pension savings would. (Reminder these figures are compared against a pension market performing at 5% compound growth per year.)

Figure 26

Minimum Gross Rental Yields Required

Repayment

10%	9.5%	9%	9.5%	9%	9.5%	8%
£50,000	£55,000	£60,000	£65,000	£75,000	£100,000	£124,500

Interest Only

10%	9.5%	9.5%	9.5%	9%	9.5%	8.5%
£50,000	£55,000	£60,000	£65,000	£75,000	£100,000	£124,500

How to Read the Diagram

The purchase price is displayed below each stylized house. The percentage figure shown in the house is the minimum Gross Rental Yield David should be looking to achieve, if he wants to out–perform a pension. You will see there are two different figures for each house value, one for a Repayment Mortgage and one for an Interest Only Mortgage. In most cases these are the same, where they differ it is because we are looking to exceed the £18,000 income target and this may mean purchasing an additional property. We will learn more about this in the next few Chapters.

General Rule for Investing: As a Rule of Thumb you can see that the Gross Rental Yield required to deliver a saving against additional pension contributions, is 3% – 4% above the Mortgage interest rate (remember all the modelling calculations were based on a 6% interest rate). If you can secure a Gross Rental Yield which exceeds this level the savings you can achieve are even greater.

Looking at the diagram you can see that if David were to purchase a property at £60,000 he would require a minimum Gross Rental Yield of 9% if bought on a Repayment mortgage and 9.5% if bought via an Interest Only Mortgage.

Purchasing properties at these Gross Rental Yields will allow David to achieve his aim of filling his pension income shortfall of £18,000 pa, while spending less of his own money.

So the next logical question to ask would be "are these Gross Rental Yields realistic?" Do they translate to monthly rentals that can be achieved? The table below illustrates the monthly rental values David needs to be looking for to know with confidence that he has purchased property which will give him a superior solution than his pension.

Figure 27

Monthly Rental Required			
Purchase Price	**Mortgage Type**	**Gross Rental Yield**	**Monthly Rental Required**
£50,000	Repayment	10%	£417
	Interest Only		
£55,000	Repayment	9.50%	£435
	Interest Only		
£60,000	Repayment	9%	£450
	Interest Only	9.50%	£475
£65,000	Repayment	9.50%	£515
	Interest Only		
£75,000	Repayment	9%	£563
	Interest Only		
£100,000	Repayment	9.50%	£792
	Interest Only		
£124,500	Repayment	8%	£830
	Interest Only	8.50%	£882

From my experience in Nottingham many of these figures are achievable, and in several cases can be exceeded. For example I have purchased houses at £60,000 which deliver a monthly rent of £500 (On current LHA figures this would be £511 per month).

Note: You will have probably noticed that I have concentrated on house purchases which are below the Stamp Duty threshold of £125,000, this is because the lower priced houses are able to deliver higher Gross Rental Yields overall. As we only have 16 years to fill David's pension shortfall, rental return is of paramount importance.

One of the reasons I have included a Hands Free / Sourcing fee into the calculations is because I recognise houses of these low values may not be on your doorstep. We will cover this in more detail later in the book.

The most important message to understand however, is that for investment purposes **'not all property is the same'**.

Investing in property to fill your Pension shortfall is not simply about purchasing the property you like, it's about making informed, controlled and purposeful decisions. Sixteen years to turn your future around isn't long. However, based on these Gross Rental Yields there is capacity to spend less than £271,400, to cover all the property expenses we detailed and deliver a retirement income of £18,000 pa+

So the natural next question is ...

16. How much can you save by Investing in Property?

We already know from our calculations that David would need to contribute £271,400 to his pension over 16 years to generate the £18,000 income he requires in retirement. If however David chooses to invest in Property, at the identified Gross Rental Yields, what savings could he make compared to a pension? Are they significant?

The figures below capture the projected savings that David could achieve by leveraging Property investment to build his retirement income. These savings are based on a small portfolio of properties (we will discuss how many in Chapter 20) purchased with either Repayment or Interest Only Mortgages.

Figure 28

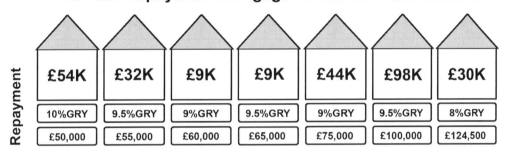

Total Savings at Breakeven Gross Rental Yields
16 Year Repayment Mortgage v Pension Contributions

£54K	£32K	£9K	£9K	£44K	£98K	£30K
10%GRY	9.5%GRY	9%GRY	9.5%GRY	9%GRY	9.5%GRY	8%GRY
£50,000	£55,000	£60,000	£65,000	£75,000	£100,000	£124,500

Figure 29

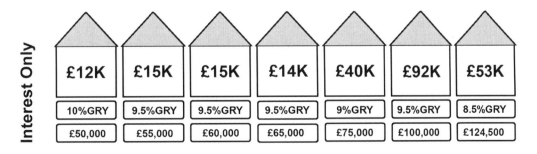

Total Savings at 'Breakeven' Gross Rental Yields
16 Year Interest Only v Pension Contributions

£12K	£15K	£15K	£14K	£40K	£92K	£53K
10%GRY	9.5%GRY	9.5%GRY	9.5%GRY	9%GRY	9.5%GRY	8.5%GRY
£50,000	£55,000	£60,000	£65,000	£75,000	£100,000	£124,500

How to Read the Diagrams

The figures shown on the previous page are the savings David can make by utilising a property portfolio (taking all our identified costs into account) to fill his pension shortfall, versus the additional cost of addressing his shortfall via topping up his pension further.

For example: If David were to purchase properties at £60,000 which delivered a Gross Rental Yield of 9% on a Repayment Mortgage and 9.5% on an Interest Only basis, he could save £9,000 and £15,000 respectively over the 16 year period.

Remember the figures above are based on the 'breakeven' points (or as close as we can get to them, based on the size of one house as 'one unit' and our mortgage costs @ 6% interest rates). If however, David were able to purchase £60,000 houses which delivered a Gross Rental Yield of 10% the savings rise significantly, as shown in the graphic below.

Figure 30

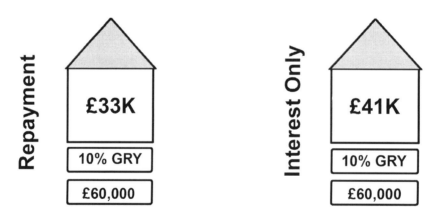

As this demonstrates there are significant savings to be made over the mortgage term. However, you do need to stay realistic, the lower the Gross Rental Yield the greater the chance of such a yield being achievable.

The next two figures illustrate the Property savings on the 'breakeven Gross Rental Yield' as a percentage versus the pension contributions.

Figure 31

Percentage Savings at 'Breakeven' Gross Rental Yields
16 Year Repayment Mortgage v Pension Contributions

Repayment						
20%	**12%**	**3%**	**3%**	**16%**	**36%**	**11%**
10%GRY	9.5%GRY	9%GRY	9.5%GRY	9%GRY	9.5%GRY	8%GRY
£50,000	£55,000	£60,000	£65,000	£75,000	£100,000	£124,500

Figure 32

Percentage Savings at 'Break Even' Gross Rental Yields
16 Year Interest Only v Pension Contributions

Interest Only						
5%	**6%**	**6%**	**5%**	**15%**	**34%**	**19%**
10%GRY	9.5%GRY	9.5%GRY	9.5%GRY	9%GRY	9.5%GRY	8.5%GRY
£50,000	£55,000	£60,000	£65,000	£75,000	£100,000	£124,500

If we were to take the same example as earlier and David purchases a £60,000 house with a 10% Gross Rental Yield (so 0.5%– 1% above the 'Breakeven yields' identified) there is a significant increase in percentage savings on offer.

Figure 33

Percentage Saving at 10% Gross Rental Yield Properties costing £60,000 v Pension Contributions

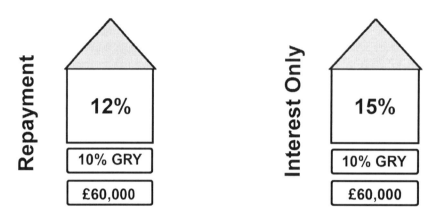

What our analysis proves clearly is that investment in the right type of property can out–perform a Pension in terms of the personal cost to you, i.e. Property investment requires less of your money to fill your pension shortfall over the 16 year term, even allowing for all the associated costs.

So in terms of Figure 34, our ultimate solution we can confirm that Property investment is on the Right Hand Side of the Chart, but we now need to establish whether it is sitting within the 'Bottom RH box' or 'Top RH box' ?

Remember our aim is to achieve the Top Right Hand Corner, by demonstrating not only can Property investment cost you less to address your pension shortfall, but it can also 'outperform' the pension by delivering you 'more income'.

Figure 34

Four Possible Property Outcomes

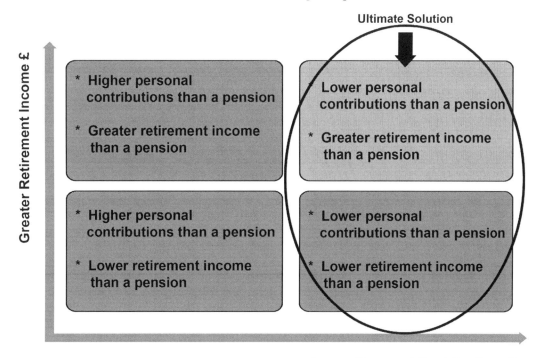

So the next question to ask is…

134

17. How much more Retirement Income will Property Deliver?

As we know our target is to fill David's £18,000 Pension Shortfall, and we have already compared the contributions he would be required to make into his Pension against the cost of building a property portfolio. Figure 35 over the page now shows our projected rental income, based on our Breakeven Gross Rental Yields.

This retirement income has been based on David reaching 65 and having the required number of properties unencumbered (and on the rental income growing by 2.5p% pa). This means on a Repayment Mortgage the last payment has been made, and on an Interest Only basis houses have been sold to clear the debt on the remaining properties.

In all cases the solution has been based on the same number of houses in retirement, hence in most cases the projected income is the same irrespective of whichever mortgage route has been followed. Where it differs it is because a greater rental yield was required when following the Interest Only route to reach our desired target of £18,000.

One of the first things to notice is that almost all options have the potential of producing more income than putting additional money into a pension fund at 5% compound growth. This means they will produce a retirement income which exceeds £18,000. Why is this?

As previously mentioned, houses are big units, so unlike putting additional money into a pension where the contributions can be increased by units as low as £1, you are unable to purchase part of a house. In our desire to hit the target of David's pension shortfall, sometimes it has meant purchasing an additional property, when actually only 40% is required. The resulting benefit is, of course, increased rental income.

Another feature to consider is that when seeking the 'breakeven' Gross Rental Yields, our calculations have increased in 0.5% increments. So the true 'breakeven' GRYs sits somewhere between the first yield that indicates a saving and the yield below, i.e. If 9.5% shows a saving the true breakeven point is between 9% and 9.5%.

The calculations over the page represent projected Retirement Net Income (before Tax) taking into consideration the comprehensive on–going property costs we have allowed for and the Breakeven Gross Rental Yields we have said David needs to achieve.

Figure 35

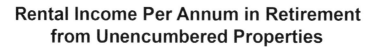

How to Read this Diagram

Along the bottom of the diagram you will see the purchase price of each property within the portfolio and the Gross Rental Yield. The Annual Rental Income achievable is shown before tax.

It is important to understand, this retirement income sits completely outside any influence from annuity rates, interest rates or house price fluctuations. This makes it an extremely powerful and reliable retirement income.

At this stage, the properties are unencumbered.

The additional income achieved as a percentage of our target income is shown in the graphic over the page.

The −1% showing against the £50,000 portfolio is due to achieving an projected retirement income of £17,857 pa (i.e. £143 pa short of our target), it seemed overkill to purchase an additional house to make up such a small difference.

Figure 36

Additional Retirement Income Received from Property as a Percentage of Pension Target

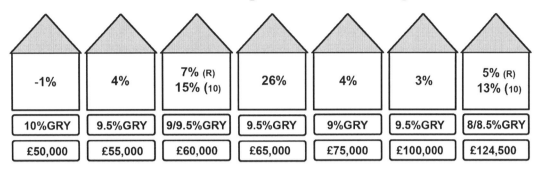

-1%	4%	7% (R) 15% (10)	26%	4%	3%	5% (R) 13% (10)
10%GRY	9.5%GRY	9/9.5%GRY	9.5%GRY	9%GRY	9.5%GRY	8/8.5%GRY
£50,000	£55,000	£60,000	£65,000	£75,000	£100,000	£124,500

How to Read this Diagram

The percentages represent how much more money David would have in his pocket over and above our target of £18,000. So for example a portfolio of properties costing £65,000 and delivering a Gross Rental Yield of 9.5% would provide 26% more retirement income than the pension option.

The results have proved that even allowing for all the associated property costs, which remember includes paying for both a Buy to Let Mortgage and a Residential Remortgage) it's possible to achieve David's ultimate retirement solution of:

- Filling his Pension Shortfall while spending less money than increased pension contributions would require
- And in most cases gaining significantly more retirement income than the projected pension income after 16 years additional contributions.

And **importantly** all this can be achieved via a route which offers reduced risk and increased certainty.

So the question is 'Why do so many people sit on the fence rather than taking the leap of faith into Property investment?'

Is it because people fear the unknown and listen to all the negative comments in the press, or is it because, in our instant gratification society, it is difficult to see beyond the 'here and now' to that place where the savings become more obvious?

Bearing this in mind the next Chapter will help you understand how quickly the savings can be realised.

18. How Quickly Can Savings be Realised?

Before we start to look at this, it would be good to remind ourselves that in all our calculations the on–going costs have increased with inflation at 2.94% per year and the rent has increased by an average of 2.5% per annum.

Based on this, the relationship between the Mortgage payments and all other costs changes over time. Although, the erosional power of inflation on real mortgage debt cannot remove the debt it can have a dramatic effect on the financial results.

If you knew you would save considerable money over the longer term, even if in the shorter term you had to spend slightly more, you would still take action in the knowledge it was a wise business investment. There is after all the saying "you have to speculate to accumulate".

So if the monthly contributions to his property solution are not immediately lower than the pension option how long does David have to wait, before the cost of running a property portfolio (accounting for all identified costs) drops below the pension contributions?

Figure 37 below, is based on a Repayment Mortgage and compares David's Pension contributions to our 16 Year Property plan.

Figure 37

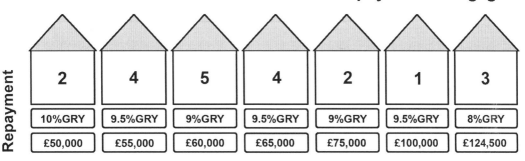

Number of Years until Property Costs are lower than
Pension Contributions - Based on Repayment Mortgage

How to Read this Diagram

The figures in the houses represent the year in which the property portfolio costs become less than the pension contributions.

As you can see the switch in favour of property happens early in the 16 year mortgage term and in many cases actually within the first four years of the mortgage term. The Interest Only BTL Mortgages show a similar positive outcome, although slightly longer in some cases (Figure 38 below).

This means the requirement for David to 'keep the faith' that he has made the right decision long term only needs to be maintained for a relatively short period of time.

Figure 38

Number of Years until Property Costs are lower than Pension Contributions - Based on Interest Only Mortgage

5	6	5	5	4	2	3
10%GRY	9.5%GRY	9.5%GRY	9.5%GRY	9%GRY	9.5%GRY	8.5%GRY
£50,000	£55,000	£60,000	£65,000	£75,000	£100,000	£124,500

To prove this point further, let's drill down into the example of £60,000 houses on Repayment Mortgages. We know that Year five is the switch year where property costs drop below pensions costs, but in the preceding four years how much extra has David paid from his own pocket to support the property option? And when will David be in a stronger financial position overall?

The table over the page is based on a Gross Rental Yield of 9% and a Repayment Mortgage Strategy. On this basis you can see David will need to find an additional 24% (over and above the pension contribution) in Year 1, 11% in Year 2 and 5% in Year 3. Year 4 the payment will be equal to the pension contribution. As we know the savings materialise in Year 5.

As the first three years may overstretch David, he may wish to consider either releasing a little more capital to cover these additional payments, or actively plan to utilise some of his £21,000 bank savings during this initial period.

Figure 39

£60,000 Purchases at GRY 9% on a Repayment Basis **Property Payments Compared to Pension Contributions over the 16 Year Term**			

Year	Property Payments v Pension Contributions	Year	Property Payments v Pension Contributions
1	24% More	9	24% Less
2	11% More	10	28% Less
3	5% More	11	32% Less
4	Equal	12	36% Less
5	5% Less	13	40% Less
6	10% Less	14	44% Less
7	15% Less	15	47% Less
8	19% Less	16	51% Less

From Year five his property costs reduce significantly and by Year 16 David's monthly payments are 51% lower than the required pension contributions.

Most importantly not only has David spent less in this scenario but at the end of Year 16 David will have guaranteed unencumbered properties. If he had chosen the route of greater pension contributions his accumulated savings would still be exposed to the Stock Market and fluctuations in annuity rates, both of which he has no control over.

The table below demonstrates the same scenario, but with David choosing to follow the Interest Only Mortgage route. Note the Gross Rental Yield required is now 9.5%.

Figure 40

£60,000 Purchases at GRY 9.5% on an Interest Only Basis **Property Payments Compared to Pension Contributions over the 16 Year Term**			

Year	Property Payments v Pension Contributions	Year	Property Payments v Pension Contributions
1	51% More	9	33% Less
2	24% More	10	40% Less
3	15% More	11	47% Less
4	6% More	12	53% Less
5	2% Less	13	60% Less
6	10% Less	14	66% Less
7	18% Less	15	72% Less
8	26% Less	16	78% Less

The key difference with the Interest Only option is:

- Initially the costs are significantly higher
- Then the savings become more pronounced
- However, at the end of the 16 years David will still have mortgage debt outstanding on each property

So in summary our calculations have established the following facts:

- On a portfolio of £60,000 properties David has the opportunity to save either £9,000 (Repayment basis Figure 28) or £15,000 (Interest Only basis Figure 29) compared with Pension contributions. At the same time generating a retirement income of £19,207 (Repayment) or £20,700 (Interest Only) (Figure 35) both in excess of our target.

- In the initial years the payments may be higher but after only a few years the swing is in favour of Property and by the end of the term the savings are considerable when comparing Property costs with Pension contributions.

However, it's important to share the complete picture and understand the cumulative 'breakeven point' in years, taking into consideration all the payments. i.e. the point when David is better off overall allowing for having had to spend more in the initial years to benefit in the later years.

Figure 41 below, illustrates that, allowing for all the costs of a Repayment Mortgage and comparing the properties' performance against a pension growing by 5% per annum, David's cumulative 'breakeven' point based on 9% Gross Rental Yield is actually at Year 13.

However, if David were to purchase properties where the Gross Rental Yield is increased to 10% this lowers the number of years dramatically and it would take only 3 years until overall he is financially better off than contributing to a pension.

Figure 41

£60,000 Properties Cumulative Savings
Property v Pension (Repayment)

The overall breakeven years follow a similar pattern with the Interest Only route.

In conclusion

We have proved that the ultimate solution can be achieved over 16 years and property can outperform the traditional pension route, even allowing for significant contingency in the interest rates utilised in our calculations and covering all property costs and two mortgages.

However, we have been realistic and understand those looking to build property into their Retirement Rescue Plan who have a limited window of opportunity time–wise, (i.e. in David's case 16 years) need to be prepared to commit to supporting slightly higher costs in the short term, for the greater good of achieving significant savings in the longer term.

To re–iterate Gross Rental Yield is the key to success.

Figure 42

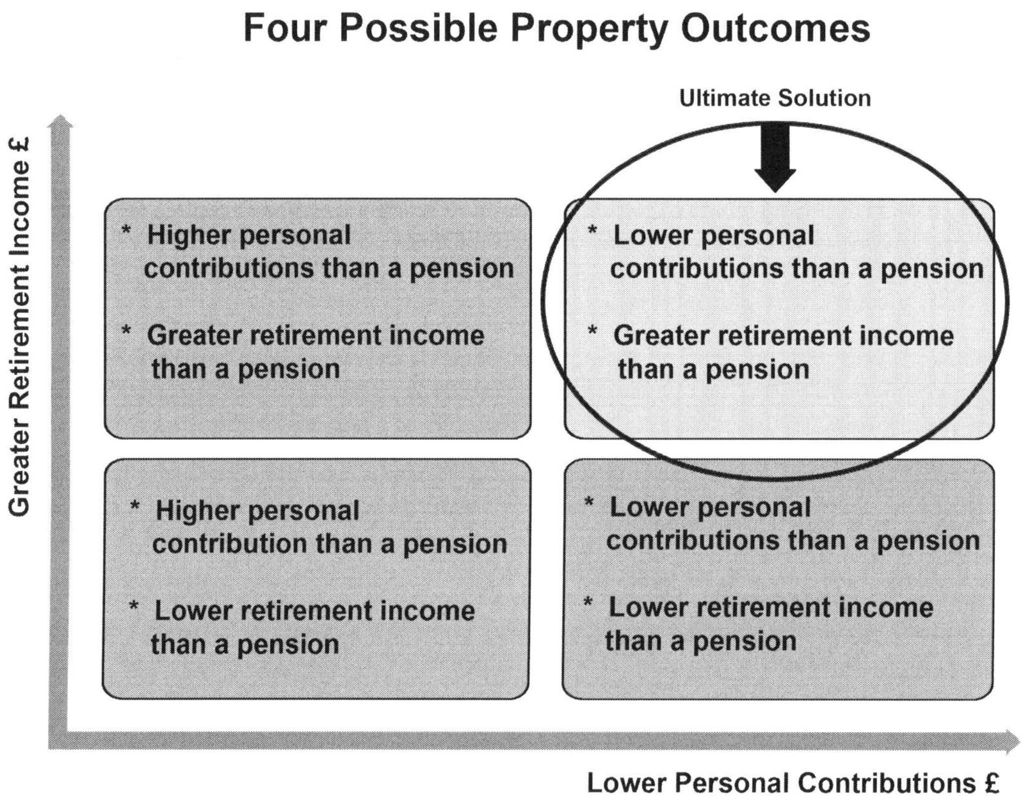

Four Possible Property Outcomes

19. What Happens if Interest Rates Go Up?

David feels confident he now understands how property investment can bring a diversified strength to his retirement planning, and provide the survival plan that he is seeking to fill his Pension shortfall.

However, he is keen to complete thorough due diligence before he starts on the strategy and he would particularly like to address the nagging question in his mind
.

'But what if interest rates go up?'

David looks back at all the costs which have been included in the financial model and he is comfortable that there is considerable contingency already built in to the mortgage interest rates. As we know all the calculations to date have been worked on an interest rate of 6% for both the Residential remortgage and the Buy–to–Let mortgage.

As a recap the tables over the page illustrates 6% is considerably higher than the current Buy–To–Let and Residential Mortgage rates on offer and contingency has already been built in for interest rates rises.

It's also possible to see the degree of contingency allowed for on the Residential Offset Remortgage is greater than the Buy–to–Let mortgage.

Why is this?

Because, as already stated, 6% is considered a sound 'long term run rate' for Buy To Let Mortgages. They have never experienced the same dramatic changes that we have seen in the residential marketplace.

(**Note:** Rates change daily, and these examples were taken in September 2013. I would advise you to speak to your Independent Mortgage Broker to ensure you secure the most appropriate mortgage product for your circumstances)

Figure 43

Examples of Buy To Let Mortgage Rates (Purchase – First Time Landlords)			
BTL Term	**Current Interest Rate @ 75% LTV**	**Modelling Interest Rate**	**Contingency built into Modelling Calculations**
BTL – 2 Year Fixed	2.99%	6%	3.01%
BTL – 3 Year Fixed	3.99%	6%	2.01%
BTL – 5 Year Fixed	4.69%	6%	1.31%

Examples of Residential Offset Mortgage Rates (Remortgage)			
Term	**Current Interest Rate @ 75% LTV**	**Modelling Interest Rate**	**Contingency built into Modelling Calculations**
Resid – 2 Year Fixed	2.29%	6%	3.71%
Resid – 3 Year Fixed	2.64%	6%	3.36%
Resid – 5 Year Fixed	3.29%	6%	2.71%

The graphs over the page illustrate visually the contingency we have already built into our calculations.

However, even taking these contingencies into account David feels it would also be good to stress test the model based on an interest rate of 8%.

Figure 44

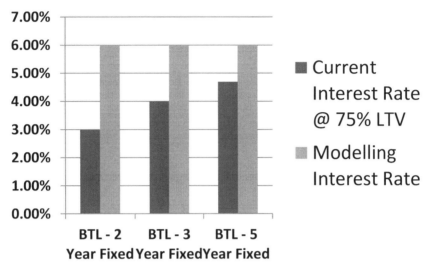

Buy To Let Mortgage Rate Examples v 6% Mortgage Rate used in Modelling Calculations

Figure 45

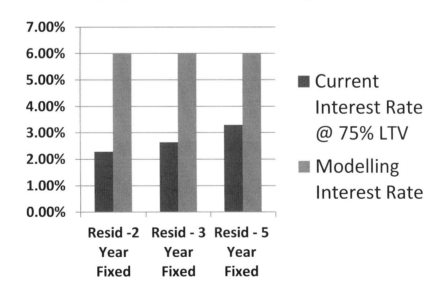

Residential Offset Mortgage Rate Examples v 6% Mortgage Rate used in Modelling Calculations

Increasing the Interest Rates to 8% for the full 16 year period will of course have a dramatic impact on the calculations.

Whereas previously the property Option outperformed the pension option the swing is now in favour of the pension scenario.

As an initial reaction, you would excuse David for being worried by these results but he, thankfully, has an understanding of economics and realises two key things.

i.   Firstly, interest rates have NEVER been at 8% for a full 16 year period. And, as the economy is so financially stretched at the moment, an interest rate rise to 8% is not sustainable and would most certainly cause the economy to go back into recession.

ii. Secondly, the pension performance has been calculated on a compound growth rate of 5% per annum. However an interest rate rise to 8% would also have a massive impact on the Stock Market. Why? Because it would increase the cost of lending to businesses which would have a correspondingly negative effect on their financial performance. Stress on financial performance would make it extremely challenging for any pension fund to deliver a consistent performance rate of 5% per annum.

In–fact the requirements of the Financial Conduct Authority (FCA) for Pension Funds to amend their projections to 2%, 5% and 8% compound growth by April 2014 is to provide a more realistic outlook to those saving for their pension. Given the circumstances of Interest Rates rising to 8% a projected growth rate of 2% may indeed be a more realistic outcome. If this were the case, to meet his £18,000 pension shortfall David would have to contribute significantly more into his fund than is currently projected so Property would again be more favourable.

Taking this into consideration David is extremely comfortable that the 8% Stress Test has proved that the property option remains a very strong rescue plan, even in this change of circumstances.

Completing this exercise has, however, been important as it has demonstrated to David that if interest rates rose from 6% to 8% (for the full period) there is significantly more financial risk associated with keeping his full portfolio on an Interest Only basis.

We have already spoken about this but the significant movement in returns shown in the graphics over the page compared to those of Figures 28 and 29 (page 129) has demonstrated how exposure to rate rises can massively impact the financial returns on Interest Only mortgages.

Figure 46

Total Savings 16 Year Repayment Mortgage v Pension Contributions
Where Interest Rates = 8% and Pension Fund Growth = 2%

Repayment						
£130K	£106K	£79K	£76K	£119K	£180K	£105K
10%GRY	9.5%GRY	9%GRY	9.5%GRY	9%GRY	9.5%GRY	8%GRY
£50,000	£55,000	£60,000	£65,000	£75,000	£100,000	£124,500

Figure 47

Total Savings 16 Year Interest Only Mortgage v Pension Contributions
Where Interest Rates = 8% & Pension Fund Growth = 2%

Interest Only						
£0.5K	£8K	-£2K	-£12K	£32K	£72K	£31K
10%GRY	9.5%GRY	9.5%GRY	9.5%GRY	9%GRY	9.5%GRY	8.5%GRY
£50,000	£55,000	£60,000	£65,000	£75,000	£100,000	£124,500

The reason the Interest Only savings have been eroded so dramatically in our 8% calculations is due to the fact that with the Interest Only model you need to proactively purchase additional houses, (so that on selling a predetermined number to clear all mortgage debt, the remaining rental income meets or exceeds the Pension Shortfall).

More houses on an Interest Only basis when rate rises occur means more financial exposure, it is as simple as that. Although Repayment Mortgages may not be deemed as 'tax efficient' from a retirement viewpoint – peace of mind is of paramount importance and these figures show the truth that is often glossed over in the investment world.

And, as a Repayment mortgage reduces both the debt and the Loan to Value ratio you will be in an increasingly positive position to negotiate more competitive interest rates during the term of the mortgage. If you refer back to Figure 15 page 97 you can remind yourself just how the debt on a Repayment Mortgage reduces over time.

Take a look at Year ten – the outstanding debt on the Repayment Mortgage has dropped to £24,995, while the Interest Only option remains at £45,000. It's that additional £24,000 of borrowing per property which costs more when rates rise.

In addition to having your portfolio either fully or partly on a Repayment basis, fixing your mortgage for a period of years will also help reduce your exposure to rate rises.

So, in summary if you're worried about interest rate rises and how you would cope, I would recommend you follow the action plan shown below:

- fix your mortgage for as long a period as possible
- opt to repay, some or all of your mortgage to reduce your exposure

20. How Many Houses Will I Need?

Now that David is keen to diversify into Property investment to meet his pension shortfall he would like to understand exactly how many houses he requires in his portfolio.

You have probably guessed by now that the simple answer is, "It depends!"

It depends on two key factors:

- The Gross Rental Yield achieved
- The Mortgage Strategy adopted (Repayment or Interest Only)

This is because:

- Higher Gross Rental Yields = Less Houses Required
- Repayment Mortgages = Less Houses Required.

As we know the whole emphasis of this book is to help David establish a retirement plan over the 16 years which meets his shortfall and, in so doing, provides maximum return for minimum risk. He already has risk associated with his pension, over which he has no control. So this chapter is aimed at explaining 'why and how many' houses are needed to achieve his financial goal.

Before we go on to this I want to reiterate that the main way to reduce risk and increase income certainty is to follow a Repayment strategy. The reason I am emphasizing this is because it goes against the norm of the traditional Property investment world. The majority of property investors purchase with an Interest Only Mortgage to increase cash flow from Day One. Often, they also churn capital out of their property after a minimum period of six months, riding the wave of inflation to erode the value of the mortgage debt. The quote 'Oh I'll sell **some** to clear the debt on others' is commonly heard.

However from a retirement planning strategy this approach brings with it some major risks, namely:

- Over–gearing your portfolio and having high exposure to interest rate rises (we have already seen the impact of this in the previous chapter).

- Having no outright ownership of your property portfolio on retirement.

In my view the 16 years we have to solve the pension shortfall for David isn't long enough to benefit from the full power of inflationary erosion of mortgage debt. As I've already stated, it takes 24 years to halve the 'real value' of debt, when inflation runs at 2.94% pa and David doesn't have 24 years!

The whole purpose of this book is to help you understand 'why' it is necessary to take action and control of your retirement planning and then to provide proof that Property investment can be a successful route to achieving your goals. It's important to me that I provide the full picture as best I can, so that 'informed decisions' can be made. Having the facts on the table allows proactive decisions to be made which meet personal requirements.

Ultimately it is David's choice (just as it is yours) as to which route he follows to achieve the endpoint, but in making his decisions it is important that he fully understands the ownership issue.

Taking the example of a £60,000 house on a Repayment Mortgage versus an Interest Only Mortgage, (with house prices increasing at 2.8% per annum), at the end of the 16 year Mortgage Term the purchaser on the Repayment Mortgage will have 100% ownership and no debt, while the purchaser on the Interest Only Mortgage will have only 52% ownership plus £45,000 of debt. A noticeable difference.

Retiring at 65 years old with outstanding debt of £45,000 on each investment property would leave David exposed to any change in the Bank's lending criteria. This may mean he is prevented from remortgaging past a certain age, (certainly during the financial crisis 75 years was the usual limit), so he would need a pre–determined plan for clearing his debts.

He would also have continued exposure to interest rates and house prices, at a time when he should be seeking 'certainty' in his life, and he would receive less 'monthly retirement income' than his Repayment counterpart, as he would still be paying a mortgage.

Never has it been truer to say you need to "start with the end in mind"

The table on page 154 (Figure 48) helps to illustrate the point.

In David's case we know we need to fill a pension shortfall of £18,000, so we can work backwards to ascertain how many unencumbered houses are required in retirement.

With the Interest Only route after 16 years, we now know, the level of ownership of each property is approx. 52%. So it would appear that selling approximately half of the portfolio would clear the debts on the remainder. Unfortunately it's not quite so straightforward as Capital Gains Tax will be due on each sale based on any increase in value since purchase.

A Tax Accountant will be able to advise on Capital Gains Tax in a specific circumstance but, for the purposes of this book, I have used the HRMC website (www.hmrc.gov.uk) to document in Figure 49, the basic principles used to calculate Capital Gains Tax.

The message is clear if you are planning to sell any properties it's important that you take Capital Gains Tax into consideration. Failure to do so could leave you painfully short of the money you thought you had available to clear debt and the income you thought you had to live on.

Figure 48

Repayment v Interest Only – Property Ownership

| | | £60,000 House | | | |
| | | Repayment Mortgage | | Interest Only Mortgage | |
Year	House Value	Outstanding Debt at the Start of each year	% Ownership of House	Outstanding Debt at the Start of each year	% Ownership of House
1	£60,000	£45,000	25%	£45,000	25%
2	£61,680	£43,271	30%	£45,000	27%
3	£63,407	£41,436	35%	£45,000	29%
4	£65,182	£39,487	39%	£45,000	31%
5	£67,008	£37,418	44%	£45,000	33%
6	£68,884	£35,222	49%	£45,000	35%
7	£70,813	£32,890	54%	£45,000	36%
8	£72,795	£30,414	58%	£45,000	38%
9	£74,834	£27,786	63%	£45,000	40%
10	£76,929	£24,995	68%	£45,000	42%
11	£79,083	£22,033	72%	£45,000	43%
12	£81,297	£18,887	77%	£45,000	45%
13	£83,574	£15,548	81%	£45,000	46%
14	£85,914	£12,003	86%	£45,000	48%
15	£88,319	£8,239	91%	£45,000	49%
16	£90,792	£4,243	95%	£45,000	50%
17 Retirement	£93,334	£0	100%	£45,000	52%

Note: The calculations have been based on Real House Values increasing by 2.8% pa. Data source Nationwide Building Society Q1 1975 to Q1 2013.

154

Figure 49

Working Out Capital Gains Tax

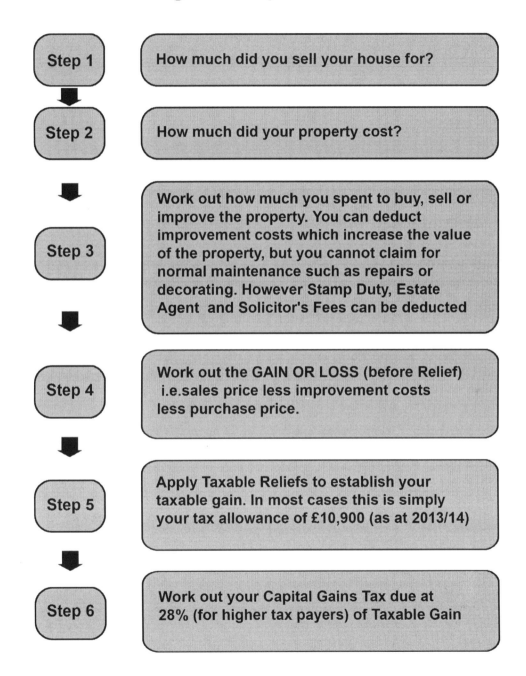

Step 1 — How much did you sell your house for?

Step 2 — How much did your property cost?

Step 3 — Work out how much you spent to buy, sell or improve the property. You can deduct improvement costs which increase the value of the property, but you cannot claim for normal maintenance such as repairs or decorating. However Stamp Duty, Estate Agent and Solicitor's Fees can be deducted

Step 4 — Work out the GAIN OR LOSS (before Relief) i.e.sales price less improvement costs less purchase price.

Step 5 — Apply Taxable Reliefs to establish your taxable gain. In most cases this is simply your tax allowance of £10,900 (as at 2013/14)

Step 6 — Work out your Capital Gains Tax due at 28% (for higher tax payers) of Taxable Gain

Note: Further information at www.hmrc.gov.uk/cgt/property

If we take the previous example, David's debt outstanding on a £60,000 purchase on an Interest Only Mortgage after 16 years would be still be £45,000. (In 'Real Value' this will of course seem lower, but the fact remains the full debt is outstanding).

Assuming each house has grown in value by 2.8% per annum, when he sells the property (and keeping our figures extremely simple) he is likely to have a Capital Gains Tax Bill of approx. £7,800 per property. Each year David receives a Capital Gains Tax Allowance so, working with an Accountant he could plan the sale of any houses to maximise his Allowances. However, again for simplicity in our calculations we have assumed that David sells all the houses in the same tax year, his retirement year, so is only able to take advantage of one Allowance, after–all he requires his portfolio to be debt free.

Figure 50

Example: Selling Property to clear Mortgage Debt

Per Property	
Purchase Price	£60,000
Mortgage @ 75% LTV	£45,000
House Value end of Year 16 (based on 2.8% growth pa)	£93,334
Market Value of all properties	£840,006
Outstanding Debt on all properties	£405,000
Approx. CGT – sell 50% of properties	£38,949

Number of Houses	
Unencumbered Properties left in Portfolio	4
Number of properties sold	5
No of properties to buy	9

The previous table illustrates how, if David required the income from four houses to fill his pension shortfall, he would actually need to purchase at least nine properties and sell five on retirement to clear the mortgage debt on the remainder (given his 16 year window). In our calculations in terms of Capital Gains Tax we have kept our calculations simplistic and have calculated the tax due based on David having to sell half his portfolio. In this example you can see the CGT bill is approximately £39,000.

Even with our simplistic figures it is important to reiterate if you are going to follow this strategy **Capital Gains Tax needs to be planned for!**

Based on a 16 year window, the graphic below provides an overview of how many houses David would need to purchase based on house values, our breakeven Gross Rental Yields and financing options. As you will see the number of houses required in a portfolio purchased via Repayment mortgages is refreshingly realistic and certainly achievable. And an achievement of higher Gross Rental Yields would of course reduce the number of houses required to hit our target income.

Figure 51

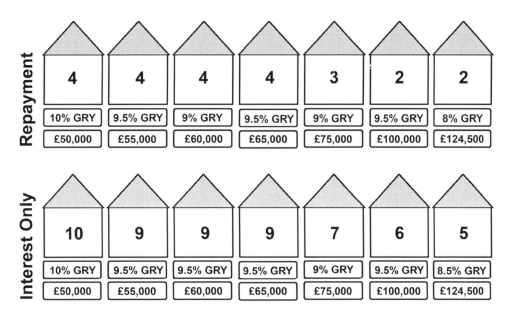

Number of Houses Required in Portfolio - Repayment & Interest Only

Creating an Asset Base

At this point it would be highly remiss to ignore the fact that once David has unencumbered houses he will have built for himself an asset base worth hundreds of thousands of pounds. And unlike a pension this asset base will not disappear with his death, but can be passed to future generations.

The graphic below projects the value of David's asset base at the end of year 16, assuming that he owns the number of properties shown and all mortgages are cleared. These projections have been based on the housing market growing at 2.8% pa over the 16 year period.

As you will see David will own a sizable asset base and therefore will be in a great position of strength.

Figure 52

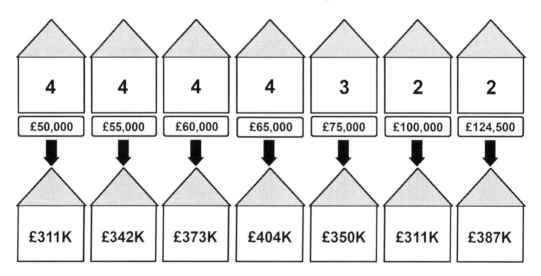

Projected Capital Value of Portfolio of Unencumbered Properties

Buying Below Market Value

I do recognise however that so far, at no point within this book have we discussed purchasing houses at a price below the normal market value of the property, even allowing for refurbishment work to be completed. Achieving this establishes "equity" from Day One and can certainly influence the number of houses needing to be sold to clear mortgage debt at the end of the 16 year term and the value of the asset base created.

Achieving this is a distinct bonus so we will discuss this more in Chapter 23.

25% Tax Free Cash

In addition, we have also failed to mention David's right to receive 25% of his pension fund as a 'tax free' payment on retirement. Since receiving tax free money is highly advantageous, you may be wondering why I haven't allowed for this in my calculations!

The reason I have omitted this pension benefit is because we are focusing on filling a pension income shortfall, and although receiving 'tax free' money is attractive it doesn't come 'free' and has to be paid for somewhere along the line. This tax free payment results in lower pension income for life, as the fund value which is converted to an Annuity is of course worth 25% less, (assuming the full tax free allowance is taken). Many people forget this fact!

So if I were to suggest this option, the additional contributions required to boost the Pension over the 16 years would need to be even higher. Only this would ensure the remaining funds could produce the income level David requires.

Since my focus has been to promote a realistic comparison between a pension and property investing, by opting to take no tax free cash the property option has been compared to the lowest level of pension contributions possible to fill the income shortfall.

Finally in concluding this Chapter, the table overleaf summarises the points we have discussed and the elements that David needs to consider. After–all we have shown the financial strategy selected will have a big influence on the risks involved and on the number of properties required on route to retirement.

Figure 53

Summary of Key Facts to Consider

Repayment Risk	
1	Interest Rate Rises
2	Voids

Interest Only Risks	
1	More houses required in the 16 Year Period
2	Greater exposure to Interest Rate Rises
3	Voids
4	House Value not at desired level when it's time to sell
5	Government Changes to Capital Gains Tax Rules eg. lower Individual Allowance
6	Inflation doesn't erode the 'real value' of the mortgage debt at the rate projected

21. How Much Seed Capital do I Need?

By now it will have become obvious that David will require investment seed capital to follow the Rescue Plan discussed in this book. This capital needs to be available as 'cash', as it can't be raised via a Buy–To–Let Mortgage.

If you refer back to Figure 24 on Page 119, you can remind yourself of the expenses included in our property calculations. All mortgage calculations are based on 75% Loan To Value Ratio which I would recommend as a retirement strategy (since it provides an equity buffer and reduces your risk). However, if you wish to borrow at a lower Loan To Value ratio you can, of course, do this. It will mean you require more capital at the outset but you will benefit from improved cash flow.

Keeping to our 75% LTV calculations the total capital required to follow the property investment strategy, is shown over the page.

The wide variation in the initial capital required, together with the risks we have already discussed and summarized in the table at the end of the last chapter (Figure 53), may well be an influencing factor in your choice of which investment strategy to follow.

Not only does the Interest Only route have more associated risks, but as you have probably already realised it requires almost double the seed capital of the Repayment strategy, if you are looking to achieve a debt free portfolio in retirement. As such it is important you are fully committed to this strategy and understand its downside, if you wish to benefit from the additional financial savings it has the potential to offer.

Figure 54

Initial Capital Required for Investment Strategy

Repayment						
£108K	£113K	£118K	£123K	£101K	£80K	£94K
10% GRY	9.5% GRY	9% GRY	9.5% GRY	9% GRY	9.5% GRY	8% GRY
£50,000	£55,000	£60,000	£65,000	£75,000	£100,000	£124,500

Interest Only						
£271K	£255K	£266K	£277K	£237K	£240K	£236K
10% GRY	9.5% GRY	9.5% GRY	9.5% GRY	9% GRY	9.5% GRY	8.5% GRY
£50,000	£55,000	£60,000	£65,000	£75,000	£100,000	£124,500

In terms of raising the capital to invest there are three main options:

- **Option 1:** 100% from savings
- **Option 2:** A mixture of savings plus equity raised from your residential home
- **Option 3:** 100% from equity raised from your residential home

Option 1: represents the cheapest financial option as it only costs the loss of bank interest. As we learnt in Chapter 8 *'What if you have Money in the Bank?,* the average deposit interest paid in 2011 was only 2.75%, which is considerably lower than the 6% we have used in our calculations.

In fact as I write this there is a newspaper article (June 2013) announcing that Building Societies are reducing their interest rates for savers even further, due to the Government's Funding for Lending Schemes.

Utilising savings to fund your investment could, therefore, offer a significant financial benefit. If we take the example of buying 3 x £60,000 houses with a total capital requirement of £135,000 (based on 75% LTV) the loss of interest received at 2.75% would only be £3,712pa, compared to the £8,100 interest due if the money is borrowed at 6%.

Option 3: is the most expensive option as it raises all the investment capital from remortgaging your home. This worst case scenario is the route we have deliberately adopted in our calculations, so as to demonstrate clearly that, even given the higher costs, there are still savings to be achieved with property versus a pension.

The strategic decision to utilise equity in your own home to build your pension offers you the ability to leverage your own money, and the money of other people (via the bank) to address your pension shortfall. This is a very powerful strategy.

However, it is absolutely **imperative** that this equity is repaid prior to your retirement, as our Retirement Rescue Plan is based fully on ensuring you do not take debt into retirement. This is why in our modelling calculations the re–mortgage has been calculated on a Repayment basis.

Option 2: This option will cost you somewhere between the above 2 scenarios dependent on your mix of savings to equity.

To reiterate, I have deliberately incorporated the most expensive option in my calculations to prove just how powerful Property investment can be in your pension planning process. From David's viewpoint, as he is established and has equity in his own home, he feels comfortable with the solutions offered. The solution he ultimately selects will be determined by the equity he is able to release from his home, based on his income.

What would I recommend to David?

My personal recommendation would be that David should focus his retirement strategy on the house price range £55,000 –£100,000 but only on those properties that deliver a Gross Rental Yield sufficient to ensure returns exceed pension performance. By referring back to Figure 26, page 126 David can remind himself of the yields he should be seeking.

To me there are five reasons why I would recommend this strategy to David:

Reason 1

The initial capital required is not prohibitive taking into consideration his salary, particularly if a Repayment strategy is adopted.

Reason 2

By concentrating on this price range and the Gross Rental Yields which outperform the pension, David can be guaranteed certainty in his Pension Planning, again particularly if he follows the Repayment model.

The power of this additional certainty should not be under–estimated. As a reminder, in each scenario the property expenses have been compared against a pension growing at 5% compound growth per annum over the 16 Year period. From April 2014 all Pension Fund Providers will be required by the FCA (formerly FSA) to amend their growth projections from the current 5%, 7% and 9% per annum to 2%, 5% and 8% respectively, (to provide a more realistic projection on pension fund growth). So by selecting 5% as our benchmark growth rate we are likely to match the rate most IFA's will adopt on their documentation and websites.

However, the key fact is that the 5% is fluid and only remains as a projected growth, there is absolutely no guarantee that pension funds will perform at this level, year in year out. There is also no certainty that annuity rates will not fall further.

Reason 3

As David is new to investing, renting to families is more stable, and purchasing lower priced houses will as a general rule attract higher Gross Rental Yields. As our strategy is focused on cash–flow this is a key factor.

However, lower priced housing stock has the propensity to attract tenants who require support through Housing Benefit. In fact, a large percentage of the tenants in our own portfolio in Nottingham receive Housing Benefit. These are families who would have qualified for a Council house, when there was stock available. Now they rely on Housing Associations and private landlords for a home.

It is David's Retirement Plan so ultimately it is his decision whether he's happy renting to a family who receive financial support. Tenants who receive Housing Benefit are not by default habitually unemployed – even though the press would have us believe this. To qualify for Housing Benefit you need to be on a low income, so this can include many employed people and the benefit can pay for part or all of their rent.

Through our personal experience, the truth is that you can get disrespectful tenants in all walks of life, so the best advice would be for David to work with his Letting Agent to adopt and implement stringent processes and strategies to reduce his risk.

As a reminder, below are a few actions which can be taken:

- Always take a deposit upfront (if a tenant can't afford this are they the type of tenant David wants to house?)

- Consider signing up for a Rent Guarantee policy. We have included one in all our calculations

- For added comfort David could also seek a "Guarantor". I recommend the Guarantor should be a 'Homeowner' as it provides additional stability.

- David should ensure his Letting Agent completes all the standard credit checks and character references and then, even if they pass these, if his gut feel says 'don't accept' the prospective tenant, I would recommend he listens to his instincts. They can have an uncanny habit of picking up signals the conscious mind fails to recognise.

Finally, even though flats and apartments could fall into the price range we are discussing I would recommend David stays away from leasehold properties. Why?

We are looking to stabilise David's retirement income and in leasehold properties the Ground Rent and Service Charges are set externally, so are out of his control. Over time these expenses can easily mount up and turn what is a 'good investment' into a 'bad' one.

I have heard several stories where rental income has been wiped out, or severely reduced, by rising costs. In fact in some cases it has caused the investor to try and sell but as the charges are prohibitive it has become an unattractive property to any buyer. The investor is then trapped with a property which is underperforming, but cannot be sold.

So my recommendation to David would be to make it a rule to buy freehold properties only. This way he can maintain control of his pension income.

Reason 4

From our analysis, those properties which have out–performed a pension at mortgage interest rates of 6%, also hold their own financially at an interest rate of 8% (particularly if a Repayment model is followed). Since the probability of the interest rate rising to 8% and remaining there indefinitely, is nigh on impossible these value houses provide a big safety margin, particularly if you are a nervous investor.

Reason 5

From a first glance the graphic on page 157, you might consider a portfolio of just two houses to generate the retirement income required, looks extremely attractive. However a portfolio of three to six cheaper houses would ultimately offer a far more stable solution for retirement.

If we consider this from David's viewpoint, by spreading his income across smaller units he would be reducing his risk. If we compare two examples, this will help demonstrate the principle.

By purchasing £60,000 houses at 9% Gross Rental Yield, we know David would require four houses to generate an income of £19,207 which exceeds his retirement shortfall of £18,000. This would require an equity input of £118,200.

Now if he were to choose to fill his pension shortfall via houses which cost £124,500 he would need to locate two houses with a Gross Rental Yield of 8% (assuming he is purchasing on Repayment basis) to out–perform a pension (this would be more challenging). He would however only need initial Seed Capital of £94,350 and the projected retirement income would be £18,871.

Initially the second option may seem more appealing, but remember we are looking to provide David with a retirement solution which is as financially strong as we can possibly make it. So with the £124,500 houses, not only may it be more challenging to find a Gross Rental Yield of 8%, but we must consider what happens when David experiences the inevitable void periods on his properties?

The table below clearly illustrates how four income sources offer greater stability than two, enabling risk to be spread and therefore exposure to loss of retirement income through tenancy voids is reduced.

Figure 55

Lost Retirement Income

Property Price	No Houses Required	Gross Rental Yield Required	Lost income from one empty property	Lost income from two empty properties
£60,000	4	9%	25%	50%
£124,500	2	8%	50%	100%

To my mind there is little point in following a Retirement Rescue Plan which can so easily leave you financially wanting. To me, the risk that 100% of your income may be missing in any one month is a risk that is not worth taking.

22. Where Do I Find these Houses?

So where would David find these houses priced between £55,000 and £100,000 and offering the Gross Rental Yields that are recommended?

Typically they represent 2 – 3 bedroom Terrace houses in a City / large conurbation. The table over the page has been produced using house price data from the Land Registry of England and Wales, July 2012 – Sept 2012, Rental figures taken from www.rentright.co.uk, and Local Housing payment figures from the government website.

One thing to remember is these are the 'averages' so should only act as a guide to David. The spread of house prices is likely to match the curve shown below (Figure 56).

There will always be a percentage of houses priced higher and a percentage of houses priced lower.

Figure 56

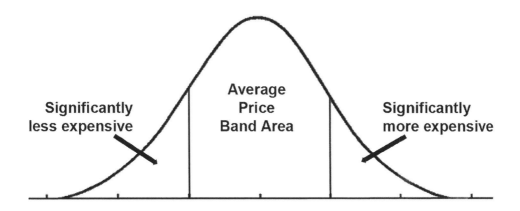

Spread of House Prices

Significantly less expensive

Average Price Band Area

Significantly more expensive

Figure 57

Location	Average House Price Terrace – July to Sept 2012	Average Rent – 3 Bedroom Property	Average Gross Rental Yield – 3 Bedroom	LHA Monthly Rent – 3 Bed	Gross Rental Yield LHA – 3 Bed
			Average Gross Rental Yields by Location		
Nottingham	£87,135	£759.00	10.45%	£500	6.9%
Actual Achieved Nottingham	£60,000			£500	10.0%
Blackpool	£78,199	£582.00	8.93%	£564	8.7%
Liverpool	£95,532	£596.00	7.49%	£525	6.6%
Birmingham	£126,429	£615.00	5.84%	£550	5.2%
Manchester	£128,364	£765.00	7.15%	£595	5.6%
Hastings	£160,434	£827.00	6.19%	£699	5.2%
Derby	£108,875	£608.00	6.70%	£500	5.5%
Leicester	£117,409	£641.00	6.55%	£550	5.6%
Crawley	£186,830	£980.00	6.29%	£925	5.9%
Luton	£141,145	£851.00	7.24%	£700	6.0%
Leeds	£129,177	£743.00	6.90%	£650	6.0%
Slough	£208,349	£1,173.00	6.76%	£960	5.5%
Bradford	£109,408	£519.00	5.69%	£475	5.2%
Reading	£207,356	£966.00	5.59%	£900	5.2%
Ashford	£165,266	£783.00	5.69%	£700	5.1%
Guildford	£281,101	£1,445.00	6.17%	£1,150	4.9%
Cardiff	£166,198	£792.00	5.72%	£650	4.7%
Maidstone	£186,893	£859.00	5.52%	£750	4.8%
Eastbourne	£191,147	£912.00	5.73%	£785	4.9%
Bournemouth	£205,300	£1,049.00	6.13%	£800	4.7%
Exeter	£215,249	£881.00	4.91%	£700	3.9%
Maidenhead	£384,904	£1,556.00	4.85%	£960	3.0%
Brighton and Hove	£339,496	£1,410.00	4.98%	£950	3.4%
Croydon	£303,219	£1,206.00	4.77%	£1,300	5.1%
Oxford	£353,891	£1,253.00	4.25%	£950	3.2%
Newcastle Upon Tyne	£171,340	£577.00	4.04%	£493	3.4%
Cheltenham	£233,004	£922.00	4.75%	£725	3.7%

Source Data: The information above is based on figures provided by the Land Registry of England and Wales for the period July to September 2012.

Average Rent 3 Bedroom Property   http://www.rentfight.co.uk/rrpi.php
LHA Rates   https://lha–direct.voa.gove.uk/search.aspx (as at March 2013)

Note: Housing Benefit Nottingham has risen to £511 per month for 3 Bedrooms (as at July 2013)

If we take Nottingham as an example, the table shows the average terrace house price as £87,135, so we would expect the majority of terraces houses to be sold around this price, with some a little more expensive and some a little cheaper. You will see on

Figure 56 if the middle of the diagram represents £87,135 then the aim would be to invest in property which sits towards the left–hand side, i.e. the cheaper side, of this large middle band.

To support this, since January 2010 I have purchased and refurbished a total of 34 houses in Nottingham of which 61% have been terrace properties. My average price has been around the £60k mark (it is now rising slightly), 31% below the 'average of £87,135', bringing my purchases nicely to the left hand side of the large middle area.

Note: you will see I have added a row to the table showing the actual Gross Rental Yields I have been achieving to date with tenants on Housing Benefit. The payment of £500 per month for a 3 Bedroom property was taken from March 2013. This has recently been adjusted to £511 per month (July 2013), so counterbalances the slight increase in house prices.

Identifying good financial investment areas involves an element of common sense and much detective work. I've ranked the locations in the table based on the rental data provided as at March 2013, but I would definitely advise you to do your own due diligence as the market is fluid.

As we know David is looking to purchase property in our recommended price band and Gross Rental Yields, so he needs to be realistic where he searches. For example, if he were to look at Maidenhead with an average house price of £384,904 and an average 3 bed private rent of £1,556 per month, the Gross Rental Yield would be 4.85%. This is significantly below our target so the house would need to be purchased at approximately £233,400, some 40% below the average.

Since Maidenhead is not a city and there is a limited supply of terraces, the ability to purchase at such a reduced rate would be challenging. As we need David to 'act now' for his retirement he needs to be realistic and identify locations where the variance between the "average" and the price he is seeking is relatively small. This will mean he has more housing stock to select from, i.e. he is purchasing in the large middle band.

Our aim is to build David a property portfolio which provides both security and financial stability, so if the right value houses aren't where he lives my recommendation is he goes to find them. This is the reason why I have allowed for a Sourcing Fee/Hands Free investment fee within our calculations. I want David to be able to go out and seek the support he needs to make his Retirement Rescue Plan a reality, confidently knowing that the figures still work. We will discuss how to identify the Sourcing / Hands Free Partner further in Chapter 28.

In the meantime, however, if David is able to invest locally, what else should he consider?

"Location, location, location" holds as true for Buy–To–Let properties as it does when purchasing your own residential home. Think about the tenants you're hoping to attract and their requirements, as these will vary dramatically.

If you are new to investing my recommendation, as you already know, is to concentrate on Single Let Family Homes (this is why all the calculations have been done on this basis). Houses Of Multiple Occupancy (HMO's) and Student Houses certainly attract the potential for higher Gross Rental Yields, but this potential comes at the cost of far greater risk and pitfalls for a new investor (i.e. Article 4, and Licensing).

In my opinion, property investment should be viewed like a game of Monopoly. You need to secure your position in the game with the green houses, before stepping up to buy the red hotels. After all, it is your future security that we are seeking to protect.

Important Note: Investing in Property for a retirement income is NOT about buying a house that you would like to live in. It's about making the right financial decisions to make your money work hard for you. The failure of first time landlords to recognise this important distinction can cost them dearly.

How to Choose a Promising Area

Invest where people want to live, don't simply be fooled by low prices on Rightmove. Visit the location, or at least utilise the technology at your fingertips and walk down the street via Google Maps. What does the area look like? Are the houses generally well kept?

I know of at least one investor who was attracted by some very low priced (approximately £40,000) housing only to find when he visited that the majority of houses were boarded up. Who would want to rent there?

Ensure the area offers your prospective tenants the facilities they require as this will increase your ability to attract a steady supply of potential tenants. Take into consideration elements such as:

- Proximity to schools
- Proximity to shops and amenities
- Transport links – both major links and local

When determining whether to invest his money in a particular location, David would do well to also look at:

- Population size – is it growing? Is it ageing?

- Whether the area attracts local major employers?

- Whether the area is in an Enterprise Zone? This Government website link details the areas: www.enterprisezones.communities.gov.uk/enterprise–zone–map/

- Does it have strong transport links? In a society where time is precious people want to be able to move around effectively and efficiently. For example the new HS2 high–speed train will reduce the journey time between London, Birmingham, and towns in the Midlands / North including Nottingham.

- Whether the area has attracted Government Funding for regeneration? i.e. is it *"up–and–coming"* or *"down and desperate"*.

- Is the area already oversupplied with housing? Is there a glut of properties which have remained empty, unable to be let for a period of time?

- Whether the properties are affordable for investors, but also local homeowners? This is a key factor to consider (and often overlooked) particularly if David is planning to follow the Interest Only strategy, as he needs to know he has not limited his market, when it comes to selling.

  A good 'Rule of Thumb' is to aim for areas where houses are 3.5 times the value of local salaries. The table overleaf takes the median salary by job for Nottingham, as provided by www.payscale.com on 13 May 2013. Applying a safe average mortgage salary multiplier of 3.5 times, you can see that the recommended house prices sit neatly within the affordability scale of locals.

This is great news as it means the housing micro–economy is not solely reliant on new outside investors.

As you would expect there are a multitude of websites which can help you do your Due Diligence and the list below is not exhaustive, but it forms a good starting point for yourself and David.

- www.rightmove.co.uk
- www.nethouseprices.com
- www.zoopla.co.uk
- www.mouseprice.com
- www.police.UK
- www.enterprisezones.communities.gov.uk

Figure 58

Median Salary by Job – UK 13th May 2013		
Job	**Median Salary Nottingham**	**Achievable Mortgage (Salary x 3.5)**
Office Administrator	£15,885	£55,598
Software Developer	£25,678	£89,873
Quantity Surveyor	£26,598	£93,093
Mechanical Engineer	£25,536	£89,376
Project Manager, Information Technology	£36,646	£128,261
Teaching Assistant	£13,000	£45,500
Marketing Manager	£24,417	£85,460

Source: www.payscale.com
Note: Individuals reporting 169,461 (40% Female, 60% Male)

Important: I would also recommend that David downloads for free the Property–Bee software found at the following website: www.property–bee.com. This software is invaluable as it works in unison with the Firefox search engine and Rightmove.co.uk and provides additional information on each property. This includes the history of activity on the property, e.g. the date and price at which it was initially marketed, any offers accepted, any changes in price and any broken sales chains.

This information is available on both the 'Sale' and 'Rental' activity on Rightmove. As well as providing you with sales data it can show the length of time a property has been marketed for tenants. Numerous properties in an area, all with long lead times to tenant means it is an area which should be avoided.

Warning:

When purchasing an investment property it can seem very appealing to find a property with a 'sitting tenant'. Should this occur, however, you would be wise to understand two key factors which should affect your investment decision.

i.   What is the current monthly rent paid? Is there any variance from the current market rent? If a sitting tenant is paying considerably below the current market rent, because the previous landlord hasn't kept the rent up–to–date, then it can be extremely difficult to enforce a large and immediate increase.

ii.   When did the tenant take up residence? Today's default tenancy agreement is an Assured Shorthold Tenancy (AST) which normally has a fixed term period of 6 months and, on expiry, automatically reverts to a Periodic Tenancy. The key advantage of an AST is that you, as the Landlord, can recover possession of the property under a Section 21 notice, so long as any fixed term has expired and the proper form of notice has been served.

Before 24th February 1997 'Assured Tenancies' were the default type of tenancy. So what is the difference between an 'Assured Tenancy' and an 'Assured Shorthold Tenancy'?

Assured Tenancies give tenants long–term security of tenure, and tenants are entitled to stay until either they agree to go, or an order for possession is obtained. You are unable to evict an "assured" tenant just because you want to, you can only do so if one of the statutory 'grounds for possession', as set out in Schedule 2 of the Housing Act 1988 apply. This means you are unable to exert full control over your investment which, as you know, is a key factor for investing.

As it is more difficult to evict such tenants, mortgage companies usually insist that all tenancies are Assured Shorthold Tenancies and for these reasons 1 would advise against purchasing a property with a sitting tenant who has an 'Assured Tenancy'.

23. Making Money on Day One

For simplicity's sake, throughout my calculations in this book, I have taken the asking price as the price paid to the vendor. However, there will always be opportunities to buy below the asking price, which means equity can be made on Day 1. This is an important concept, as it falls in line with the property saying 'You make your money on property when you buy'!

How can David maximise his opportunities to make Money on Day 1?

As an investor, David can make quick decisions and is chain free – so he shouldn't underestimate the powerful advantage this gives him! On average one in three house sales collapses because the chain has broken, so David can position himself as the answer to the Vendor's prayer.

Sometimes we forget how many links are involved in a sales chain because we see only those we are immediately connected to. But remember, unless someone somewhere along the chain is happy to make a deliberate break and go into rented accommodation, all links need to Exchange and Complete simultaneously. The standard sale transaction can therefore require the "full house" i.e. first time buyer, right through to elderly relative going into a Care Home, renting or having passed away.

Chains can be extended even further if some of the links are not as a result of upsizing or downsizing but simply moving sideways to a new location, for work, school catchments etc.

As an investor, David represents an extremely attractive proposition to the Vendor and consequently holds a powerful negotiating position.

Why is it so beneficial to secure a property at a lower price?

The obvious answer is, it will mean a smaller mortgage but equally important it will also increase the Gross Rental Yield. Remember Gross Rental Yield (GRY) is calculated as:

Annual Rent / Purchase Price x 100 %

So achieving a lower purchase price, improves the yield. To help David build the required investing relationships and knowledge, I would encourage him to concentrate on a specific area. This will ensure he is able to recognise good deals easily and quickly, and is more likely to purchase a house at a highly competitive price.

Never apply a scattergun approach to investing, as that's a mistake many make and is a sure fire way to lead to problems.

Improving Gross Rental Yield through improved rental

Buying at a lower price is one way to improve the GRY, the other is to improve the monthly rent received. As we have already discussed one of the easiest ways to achieve this is to 'add value' to your property, which means carrying out work which increases its rental capacity (and / or Capital Valuation). There are many ways to achieve this and we have already mentioned them. However, as a reminder, I have documented a few of the more popular ones below, which David may wish to consider. When he is sourcing his pension properties he would do well to determine whether he can include any of these:

A Cosmetic Refurbishment – i.e. decorating, new carpets, kitchen and bathroom replacement (if required). This 'value add' strategy is the most common and is often adopted as part of the 'Buy, Refurbish and Hold' approach to investing (this is the approach I chose to follow).

Generally speaking, a cosmetic refurbishment is more likely to increase the house value (and therefore gain you additional equity, which can be important if you are planning to remortgage or sell later) rather than increase the rent, but it will certainly make it more attractive to good tenants.

Adding an additional Bedroom – Remember UK houses are invariably valued by their bedroom count, so adding a bedroom can certainly add capital value to your property, but also importantly it can impact the rental income. In fact this is one of the most effective ways to increase your GRY. As an example we have just converted a 3 Bedroom house into a 4 Bedroom which has taken our monthly rental from £500 per month to £625 per month. This has driven our Gross Rental Yield up from 10.6% to an extremely healthy 13.8%. You need to make sure, however, that creating the extra room is not to the detriment of the rest of the house.

Adding a driveway/garage – This is another strategy which can add capital value to the property, but may also allow higher rent to be charged, particularly if the availability of a garage makes the house unique in that area. Alternatively if the garage is in a separate garage block I am aware of investors who rent the garage on a separate basis. The combined income between the house and garage is therefore higher. And, of course, in most urban areas all off street parking is a valuable bonus.

A Cautionary Note: When you add value to your property always consider the prospective tenant and local property values. Don't put ridiculously expensive fixtures and fittings into a property which is going to be rented, or where the value of the house doesn't justify the expenditure. Also, I would advise against adding conservatories etc. They may look nice but from a rental viewpoint add little additional value.

Remember don't get carried away as the ultimate investment aim is to deliver a property to your portfolio where the refurbishment cost and purchase price combined are less than the current market value of equivalent properties. Achieve this and you will have created yourself equity from Day 1.

The diagram below illustrates the point.

Figure 59

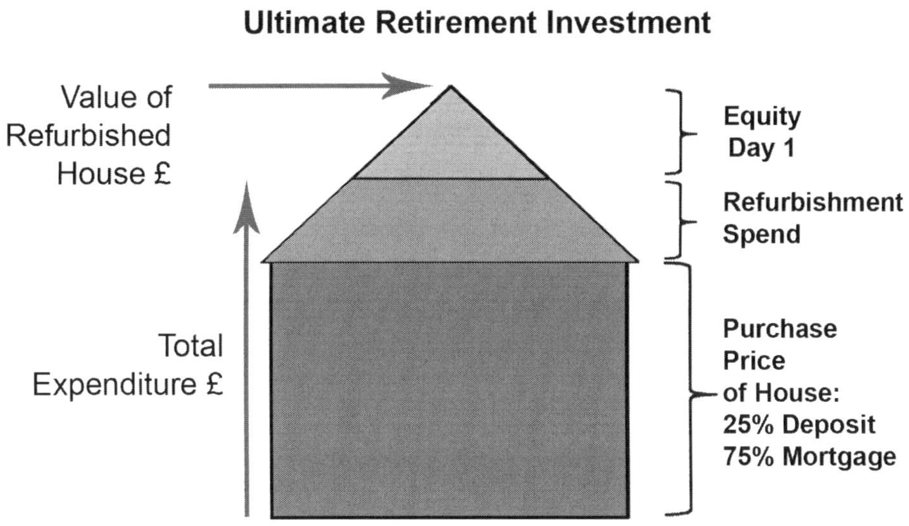

Ultimate Retirement Investment

Value of Refurbished House £

Total Expenditure £

Equity Day 1

Refurbishment Spend

Purchase Price of House: 25% Deposit 75% Mortgage

One of the key factors in achieving success is to view your property investment as a business. Purchasing Buy–to–Let properties is an un–emotional process, unlike buying your own home. Success at purchasing a sound financial investment is based on completing thorough Due Diligence, including a detailed financial review prior to purchase. This review should itemise the cost of all works to be undertaken.

To summarise, creating equity from Day 1 by 'Adding Value' to your property reduces your risk and can also offer significant additional savings to your Retirement Rescue Plan.

My recommendation

Because this is such a fundamental and important concept to grasp I would thoroughly recommend, if you're looking to source your retirement properties yourself, that you spend time gaining a solid property education before spending a penny on a house. You need to ensure your investment knowledge is worthy of committing significant capital.

Thankfully, there are numerous Property Educators promoting courses but before you sign up to anything there are two fundamental pieces of advice I would give you (we will cover this in more detail in Chapter 28).

1. Spend time upfront thinking about your preferred style – is it a large classroom environment where you can bounce ideas off others but have little opportunity for individual tuition or a one to one mentoring programme where you can receive personal coaching throughout your investment training and then be encouraged and supported as you put your training into action.

2. Be aware that many Property Educators provide one or two day 'low cost' taster courses. These are designed to impart enough knowledge to demonstrate their credibility, but normally act as a Lead Generation source for a more expensive course, where the real nuts and bolts are shared.

   As these taster courses are a sales funnel you should be prepared for incentives to be used to make you take action, there and then. If however at any time you feel uncomfortable with the approach being adopted by the Educator, I would advise you keep your Credit Card well and truly in your pocket – as they are NOT the right Educator for you!

On a personal note I established Alton Property Mentoring (previously known as Venus Property Mentoring) to work on a one to one basis with individuals, who want help and guidance on how to get started and make sound investment decisions. As the training is delivered one to one, I have the luxury of being able to tailor and mould my programmes to my Mentees' requirements, working at their own individual pace.

Uniquely each of my mentees also spends time with my Mind Coach, Alan Whitton of West Essex Hypnotherapy and Fighters Mind. This may initially sound unusual but the work my mentees do with Alan makes it so much easier for them to transform their 'investment thoughts into actions'.

24. What if House Prices Fall?

For those new to property investing, this is an understandable fear and I'm sure David would certainly have some nervousness around this area. After all if we are to believe the Press, house price crashes occur frequently and the falls are lethal for all property owners.

To help answer this question we need to view the housing market in some perspective. The housing market is cyclical and its performance is a reflection of the greater economy, this means there will be 'ups' and 'downs' and you should be prepared for this.

Let's just remind ourselves of the current cycle we are in. The Housing Market was over stimulated because the economy was strong, and there was over–zealous lending in both the United States and the UK. Mortgages became freely available, even for those who could not really afford them, and this actively boosted house prices. Then when the interest rates started to increase there was a correlating increase in defaults as those who had overstretched themselves financially felt the pain and could not sustain the higher mortgage payments. As arrears/repossessions rose, banks tightened their lending.

The economy cooled, supply outstripped demand as the basic laws of economics took effect and house prices fell. Of course there are a multitude of variants which affect house prices, but the strength of the economy/ bank lending has a fundamental influence.

Following the price correction, we have experienced a fairly stagnant market, apart from London which has a micro–climate of its own attracting foreign investment money – particularly as the Euro–crisis has identified the UK as a safe haven. However, with the various Governments Schemes recently introduced to boost lending again we are already starting to see some growth in house sales. Whether this increased activity will be sufficient to boost house prices significantly, only time will tell, (but the fact that the press is suggesting it will, will by default have an effect). As we know there are a multitude of other factors such as population growth, new build rates and an ageing population which influence house prices long term.

As we are building a Property Retirement Rescue Plan, the key message is to hold property 'long term'. In doing so, the effect of any house price 'ups' and 'downs' will be irrelevant.

Refer back to Figure 7 page 58 which illustrates the 'real' trend of house prices since 1975. If you take a closer look at the chart you can see there are distinct periods when performance was below the trend line. However, over the 30 year period (and with inflation backed out) the average growth rate has still equated to 2.8% per annum. This shows that holding your property long term really does have the ability to alleviate any fears regarding price fluctuations.

The aim is to ensure each property you purchase is financially strong, following thorough Due Diligence.

My only word of warning is that you recognise the distinction between the two strategies shown below. They are not the same in the context of a Retirement Rescue Plan and we will discuss this further in Chapter 25 'What if I don't have enough seed capital?'

- 'Buying and Holding Long Term (remortgaging only to achieve a more competitive mortgage rate); and
- 'Buying, Remortgaging (to release cash) and Holding Long term

At this stage we will just acknowledge that any re–mortgages (which release cash) need to be carried out in a calculated and controlled manner, so you can still achieve your goal of unencumbered properties in your retirement.

Going back to David, if he is still feeling a little nervous about the risk of house prices falling there are further actions he can take to reduce this risk. Before we discuss these, let's remember the purpose of this book – is to understand how Property Investment can act as an effective Retirement Rescue Plan and cost you less than a traditional pension. As part of that Plan it also provides additional 'control' – a key advantage.

So let's remind ourselves of the 'control' you currently have with your pension. Your Defined Contribution Pension savings are placed in funds where you can't personally add value and you are at the mercy of Stock Market performance, European legislation and annuity rates. In–fact the only control you have is how much money you save each month.

With Property investment you have the ability to flip this on its head and exert significant control over your retirement future, offering a massive benefit.

So recognising the housing cycle and following simple actions means David, and you, can eliminate the negative impact of any housing downturn on Retirement Planning.

The options below are designed to assist David on his journey and to ensure he feels completely comfortable that price fluctuations are manageable.

So what can David do to reduce his risk?

By following the strategy to buy for 'cash–flow' and hold long term, without remortgaging, David has immediately eliminated the effect of house price fluctuations. Too many would–be–investors do not understand this simple principle and buy for capital growth. Our focus on Gross Rental Yields is because this represents the money which you are going to live on in your retirement.

You can't live on capital growth, without remortgaging and increasing your debt. Capital growth really should be viewed purely as a bonus and property investors who forget this and think they have a Retirement Plan which will support them indefinitely can soon become unstuck.

A tenanted property with monthly rent makes fluctuations in the marketplace almost inconsequential.

In fact if you follow the Retirement Rescue Plan detailed in this book, there are only two circumstances where David may become aware of changes in house prices.

i.   The first is if he chooses to re–mortgage his property at the end of the initial mortgage term (i.e. two or three years Fixed Rate). If at this time prices have fallen, he may find himself squeezed on his Loan to Value Ratio which could limit the range of mortgages available. This risk is greater in the early years as there has been limited opportunity to increase equity and reduce debt.

ii. The second is if David opts for the Interest Only investment strategy. Having held the properties for 16 years, if the capital value takes a dip at the very time he wishes to sell to clear his debts, he may have less money than he had originally projected.

Knowing these facts, and dependent on his own risk profile, David can choose to further increase the certainty of bridging his pension shortfall by applying one or all of the following suggestions:

i.   Purchase at the right price (i.e. below current market value) and ensure there is always an equity buffer after refurbishing. This increases the protection of his physical money and the ability to re–mortgage competitively in the future. (This is where the services of a Hands Free Property Investment company could be advantageous).

ii. Follow the Repayment Mortgage strategy to reduce the debt and accelerate the improvement of his Loan to Value ratio. Should house values dip, he will still be in a position of strength regarding his mortgage.

iii.   Do not re–mortgage money out of his property until a big enough buffer of equity has been built up so that when money has been released he still has flexibility in his Loan To Value ratio. Ideally David should ensure he can support a higher Loan To Value mortgage in case the value of his house is less than anticipated. i.e. if he wishes to benefit from an 75% LTV he should be able to support an 85% LTV product in case, on valuation, he only has 19% equity in the property.

iv.   Follow the Repayment Mortgage strategy so there is no need to sell any houses and retirement income is guaranteed (subject to receiving rental income). As we know, with a Repayment Mortgage the house value at retirement will be irrelevant, and ownership of unencumbered properties will be assured.

v.   Choose a Fixed Rate Mortgage over a longer term ie three or five years. This way David will know exactly what monies are due each month.

In summary, the most important thing to understand is that Property investment offers you far greater stability than the Stock Market, even though house prices are cyclical by nature. It also provides the ability to be proactive which can eliminate, or at least significantly reduce, the impact of such changes on a Retirement Plan.

In other words, Property investment offers far greater control and certainty, even acknowledging the likelihood of house price fluctuations.

25. What if I don't have Enough Seed Capital?

On page 162 (Figure 54), we discussed the capital required to follow the investment strategies proposed in this book.

At first glance these figures may seem daunting, but remember all my calculations have allowed for the capital to be raised by remortgaging your home and repaying this loan at an interest rate of 6%, which is considerably higher than current rates.

I do realise however to gain access to this capital you need to meet two criteria:

i.   Have enough equity in your home to carry the additional debt in the short term (i.e. over the 16 years).

ii.   Have a provable income which can support this increased debt on your home.

Leveraging the money in your home to build your future is a wise wealth creation strategy and one which has been utilised by many for years. If you can access the money and use it wisely to your own good, it can be the springboard you need to turn your retirement crisis on its head. Hopefully in this book I have shown that this can be achieved in a very controlled and purposeful manner.

In fact, I would almost go so far as to say, if you are reading this book with equity in your home but inadequate pension provision, you are currently wasting a massive opportunity to improve your future. You aren't alone though – it's a common mistake of being 'equity rich, but cash poor'.

Through previous chapters we have demonstrated that investing in Property is not simply about buying the first house you like. For retirement purposes your plan needs to be detailed and specific as 16 years can pass quickly and that is all the time you have to transform your prospects in old age.

If you approach investing with care and consideration and purchase for cash–flow, Buy To Let properties can be 'assets' which put real money into your pocket each and every month. In this way they are completely different from your own home which is a liability. Understanding the difference between property as an 'asset' and property as a 'liability' is essential to understanding how Property can form a successful part of your Pension Plan.

I would recommend working with an Independent Mortgage Broker to ascertain how much equity you will be able to leverage from your home, but to get you started, in Chapter 30, I will provide you with some simple steps that you can take yourself to act as a guide.

Once you have calculated the value of the equity you can utilize, and it is still less than the amount required for the Rescue Plan of your choice, don't worry there are still options available, you just need to decide which is right for you.

So what are your options if you don't have the full amount of seed capital? Can you recycle your deposit?

One of your options is to recycle your deposit money from one property to another. This can offer the advantage of infinite returns on your seed investment, but before you embark on this route there are financial implications you must consider. I would recommend you spend time reading this Chapter, so you can make an informed decision if this is the route you wish to follow.

Advantages

- Recycling your deposit can certainly allow you to build a property portfolio from a relatively small pot of money i.e. one deposit
- Being able to remortgage all of your seed capital and refurbishment money from each purchase will deliver "infinite returns" on your capital invested, which is an extremely attractive proposition.

Note: it would be good to mention at this point, never remortgage other than to release your initial capital out of the deal. Do not be tempted to remortgage and spend the money on luxuries, as this is a sure–fire way to achieve financial misery.

Disadvantages

Although this strategy has these two significant advantages, if you are like David with only 16 years to retirement you need to review this strategy carefully, taking into consideration all the topics we have discussed in this book.

i. Firstly, to be able to implement this strategy fully and release all the deposit and refurbishment fees, each house needs to be purchased for approx. 33% less than the its normal market value.

As we know there are different ways to 'Add Value' to a property which can increase its re–mortgage value, but 33% is still very ambitious. Familiarise yourself with the Spread of House Prices graph on page 169. Remember the further you deviate from the 'Average Sale Price' the more difficult it becomes to find houses that consistently meet your requirements.

ii.   If you are new to investing it may be challenging to achieve such results, especially for the total number of houses you need, so you may find it necessary to work with a property company to take advantage of their skills / knowledge. Where houses are sourced at such big discounts there is an increased probability that creative methods of marketing, rather than the traditional Estate Agent have been used. Although these methods such as leafleting, sign written advertising vans, websites, guerrilla marketing, 'www.webuyanyhouseforcash' websites etc. are not illegal, they currently raise concerns with banks.

The bank's focus is on ensuring vendors have not been coerced into selling at a heavily discounted rate to avoid repossession etc. As you would expect, there are many reputable companies, but unfortunately, the few unscrupulous ones have tainted the bank's view. So as a word of warning it can be extremely challenging to raise a mortgage in such circumstances.

iii. If on the remortgage the valuation by the Surveyor, working on behalf of the new lender, is too low the ability to churn the full deposit and refurbishment money from one house straight to another is lost. This can halt your investment plans unless you have access to additional funds, as you will have to wait for the market to rise in your favour.

This is a big risk if you've paid a significantly large sum of money to a Property Portfolio Building Company to build a portfolio within a given number of years. I know investors who are following this strategy and it can be a real problem. The graphic over the page (Fig 60) illustrates the 'Remortgage Recycle Model'.

iv.   Remortgaging your money out of each property until you get to the last house in the chain, means you run the risk of achieving a highly geared portfolio, with only one property retaining the real equity. As we already know this will leave you increasingly exposed to interest rate rises during the 16 year period and house price fluctuations if you sell at the end of the 16 years.

Figure 60

The Remortgage Recycle Model

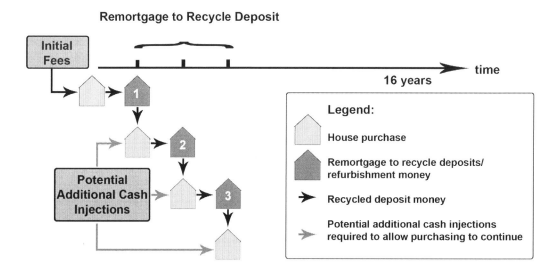

v. You are limited by the speed with which you can implement this strategy. Legally you are required to be the owner of a property for 6 months (gain 'Seasoned Title') before you can re–mortgage it. This means the absolute minimum time you can deliver a portfolio of four houses is 18 months, so if you are looking to move quicker this can be an inhibitor. Also you need to remember there will be a staggered ending of the mortgage terms, so you could be at least 68 years old before your portfolio is unencumbered (i.e. mortgage free).

vi. Significantly if you are following the Interest Only strategy, remember you will need to clear all debts to achieve your unencumbered retirement income. Also, you need to be conscious of your age, as lenders have maximum age lending limits.

vii. Some Portfolio Building Companies in particular hold a percentage ownership in the property for a given number of years. This stake of theirs in your property is often justified as 'having their skin in the deal', so ensuring it is in their interests to make it work. Although this can indeed be seen as a positive in some respects, you do need to evaluate financially what this means to you.

Gaining 100% ownership normally involves making a payment at an agreed point in the future. If, when you reach that date, you don't have the savings required you may need to remortgage again to raise the capital. Remember, every–time you remortgage you bring your debt back to current day pounds and lose that big advantage of inflation reducing debt.

In the worst case scenario this approach could lead to you remortgaging the same capital seven times in the process of building a portfolio of 4 houses. This can add several additional layers of cost, so you should go into such an arrangement fully aware of your commitment. The graphic below (Figure 61) demonstrates just how it is easy to build these additional layers of cost into your investment.

Figure 61

The Seven Potential Remortgages

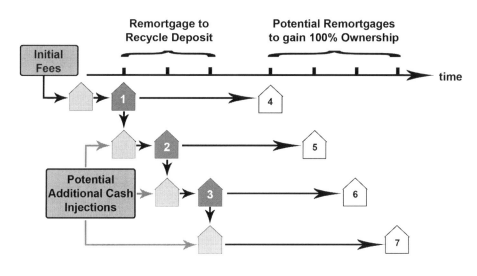

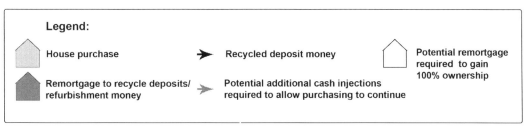

Important: The cost of buying 100% ownership needs to be included right at the outset. As it can add considerably to the overall spend.

viii. Many Portfolio Building Companies also require significant upfront fees, part of which covers the deposit for the first house. The rest covers the cost of providing their service. This can be a little deceptive if you think you are able to build a four house portfolio from one deposit, as the upfront charges can be almost as high as the value of two deposits.

What you are paying for is:

- 1 x Deposit for first house
- 4 x Service Fees upfront.

Paying the money upfront is great for their cash flow, but not so good for yours, particularly as the absolute quickest timeline with which they can deliver the full portfolio of properties is 18 months, and is more likely to be three to four years.

Most of the Property Portfolio Building companies give themselves a period of five years to deliver against their contract as they recognize it can take time to release equity and find the next house to purchase. It is certainly not a 'cookie cutter' process.

If you find yourself in the same situation as David, you don't have the luxury of waiting five years to fully implement your Retirement Rescue Plan. You need to ensure your houses are unencumbered (Repayment Mortgage) or ready to be sold to pay off mortgage debt (Interest Only Mortgage) in 16 years' time. If part of your portfolio was purchased just 11 – 12 years previous to your retirement, you are putting yourself under tremendous pressure to have enough capital to clear outstanding debts.

Note: If you do work with a Property Portfolio Building Company and pay significant upfront fees ensure your money is placed within a Solicitor's Escrow account for safety, with funds being accessed only as and when properties are delivered to your portfolio.

ix. Finally, continually remortgaging the same money and churning it from one house to another has its own 'Opportunity Cost'. You are literally paying interest on top of interest and each time you remortgage you are likely to be charged a Mortgage Arrangement Fee. All of which add up.

To summarise, utilising one deposit to build a portfolio can indeed look attractive and can support your retirement if implemented correctly, but you need to enter this type of agreement with your eyes open. I would recommend in particular you need to consider:

- Whether you have enough money to pay the upfront fees.

- Where you can find additional money en route if you find your investment 'gets stuck' and needs a cash injection to bring it back to life.

- How much it will cost you to purchase 100% ownership of the portfolio if you don't have this from Day 1, and on what date do you need to implement this.

You may find that, even though you may not have sufficient equity on Day 1 to cover the capital requirements as detailed in Figure 54 Page 162, that once you have taken time to understand the costs and implications of building a portfolio from one deposit (given your short timeline for delivery), that it's better to simply purchase a couple of houses upfront with the money you have available today. This way your 16 year clock can start ticking.

You can then add additional houses to your portfolio when you have access to further equity in your own home. Yes, these late debts might then run into your retirement, but you will have rent from two unencumbered houses to assist you, rather than having four properties with mortgages to pay.

26. Taking Action

By now you should understand the value of Property Investment as part of your Retirement Planning. As we have shown it can provide the solution to your Pension shortfall and has the potential to deliver a greater income than putting the same amount of money into a traditional Pension.

In fact diversifying into Property, to sit alongside your standard pension, brings an increased strength and dynamism to your Retirement Planning. At a time when there is so much uncertainty around pension performance, it allows you to bring 'certainty' to your future.

By investing in the 'right type' of property, you can achieve all this while spending less than would be required to generate the same income from a Pension.

So having seen the proof there really should be nothing to prevent you, or David, from taking action and following this Rescue Plan to fill your Pension Shortfall.

However, I realise that even if you have genuine worries about your retirement, and can see massive similarities between yourself and David, it's one thing knowing what you need to do and a completely different thing taking the appropriate action.

So let me emphasis how important it is that:

i.   You are fully committed to taking action in pursuit of your goal.
ii.   You decide whether you are going to complete the investing yourself or utilise the services of a Hands–Free Property Investment Company.
iii.   You follow a Step by Step Property Plan.

The remainder of this book will focus on these issues.

27. Getting Your Head in the Game

Never underestimate the power of the human brain and its innate desire to keep you safe and free from harm.

For example, even though you have read this book and seen the results, if you are new to Property investing taking action will be daunting so your natural desire may well be to stay within your 'comfort zone'. In your comfort zone the world seems a safer place and there is less risk of making a mistake.

Unfortunately however, that is not where the magic happens.

Taking action, which will take you towards the 'magic' but is beyond your peer group behaviour, takes strength of character, courage and conviction. The fear of failure is extremely common and keeps people from putting into motion exactly what is needed to become successful. Our desire to 'be liked' and 'one of the crowd' doesn't weaken as we grow up.

That being said you now understand that the majority of 'the crowd' are simply sticking their head in the sand with regard to the performance of their Pensions.

You on the other hand, understand that the pension crisis is not going to go away. You recognise that your generation is ill–prepared for retirement and that it's down to you to provide for yourself. And I am confident that having read this book you will have no desire to reach retirement regretting that you did not take action while you still had time.

Hopefully by purposefully giving you the answers to as many of your 'what if' questions as possible, this book has empowered you to take that leap of faith and start investing.

However, if you still fear change and are worried you will be taken advantage of in what you perceive to be the 'fast moving world of Property investing' you will certainly not be alone. It's natural to have nerves and if you are going to let this fear hold you back and cause you to procrastinate, then I would recommend you spend time with a Coach like Alan Whitton (www.westessexhypnotherapy.co.uk).

Coaches like Alan understand how to bring the best out of you. They help build on your strengths and confidence and work with you to help you identify the path that is right for you They also ensure that past performance or circumstances are not indicative of your future behaviour and results, and they have the ability to work with you to overcome any feelings of apprehension and inadequacy.

In fact, with just 16 years to solve a pension shortfall you could be forgiven for feeling both of these emotions, but they will not serve you well and can easily lead to procrastination. Given your relatively short timeline to implement your Retirement Rescue Plan, procrastination at this stage is no friend of yours.

You, like David, need to be acting NOW with decisive, conscious and clear actions. So if you need help focusing, or the confidence to get started, don't see this as a weakness. I would recommend you actively seek out a Mind Coach to help you 'get your head into the game'. After–all this is exactly what the professionals do, as they realise the true fight is not 'out there' but within their own mind.

'Get your Head into the Game' and you dramatically enhance your ability to deliver the performance you require.

Likewise, if you start your property journey with conviction and vigour but suffer the inevitable 'brick wall' moments, when you doubt your own abilities and everything suddenly seems like an uphill struggle, don't allow yourself to become so overwhelmed that the implementation of your Retirement Strategy comes to a grinding halt. The support of a Coach at this stage can be the exact catalyst you require to fire yourself back up.

In fact many of my successful property investing friends have visited Alan for this very reason. And on a personal note, I still regularly work with Alan so I can 'keep my head fully in the game'.

Those who are successful recognize the power of the mind and that the stronger the unison between your mind and heart, the easier it becomes to implement a Retirement Rescue Plan.

Your task is to ensure you have both elements firing on all cylinders.

28. Investing Yourself or Choosing a Hands–Free Property Partner

So once you are fully committed to the idea of Property investing you need to determine if you are going to act independently or utilise the services of a Hands–Free Property Investment Company, such as Alton Property Partners.

Invest for Yourself

If you are going to invest yourself then it's imperative that you are 100% comfortable with how to analyse and assess a good investment.

You need to become confident with spreadsheets and processes and be totally aware that purchasing property for your retirement is a business decision. An unemotional spreadsheet, backed by due diligence from websites and knowledge of the area, can help you invest quickly and decisively.

I have already expressed how important gaining a Property Education is, so understand where you have gaps in your skillset and take time and responsibility to fill those voids. There really is no excuse as there is a plethora of information readily available in terms of books, websites and courses.

If you choose to attend a course, or two – brilliant, but be mindful of ensuring you don't simply become a 'course junkie' getting your 'fix' from moving from one course to another, believing the next will provide you with all the answers (and spending considerable amounts of money en route). Education is imperative, but not at the expense of action. Remember, as long as you have the basics you can improve, refine and hone your skills as you progress.

Importantly, before you attend any courses understand what you want to learn and assess to the best of your ability, whether the course will deliver against your requirements. Call the course provider and spend time asking questions. Ideally speak to the person who will be delivering the course rather than the Sales Team, but of course this isn't always possible. However, do spend some time doing your due diligence before you part with your money. Education can indeed be costly but there is a great saying, which is very true in property;

"If you think education is expensive, try ignorance" Derek Bok

You will find there are courses and mentorships running all over the country and you don't have to part with the family silver to receive a good education.

On a personal note I established Alton Property Mentoring (aka Venus Property Mentoring) to support those new to property investing, (particularly those like you, who want to incorporate it as part of their Pension Planning) and to help them understand and master the basics. I want my mentees to feel comfortable about investing for themselves and their families.

Alton Property Mentoring offers three different programmes each of which is delivered one to one, with follow–up accountability. My mentees are able to select the programme which best meets their individual requirements and, uniquely, each programme includes one–to–one session(s) with my Mind Coach. So my mentees have the opportunity to not only master the skills of Property investing but to acquire the mindset to maximize every opportunity to reach their particular goal.

Choosing Your Educator

When you are choosing your Educator I would recommend you take time upfront to assess what you wish to achieve. The list below may help you crystallise your thoughts:

- What is your preferred style of learning? One to one or a large classroom environment. Does the educator you are speaking to match your preference?

- How confident are you that their course covers your requirements?

- Do you feel comfortable they are going to teach you (in detail) to financially analyse an investment opportunity, to calculate Gross Rental Yield, Net Rental Yield and Return on Investment?

- Is there flexibility in the programme to meet your requirements in terms of days, times etc., or is it a rigid format?

- If it spreads over several dates do you feel confident you will be able to attend all the dates?

- Will you need to take time off work to attend? If so how much and will this be possible?

- What is their process regarding follow–up calls and holding you accountable for kick–starting your investing? For example, is this offered as part of the original programme or do you need to sign up for another course?

- Do you feel they're being realistic in their projections or is there too much marketing hype, e.g. 'make a million in a month'?

- Do you know the exact cost of the programme and its content?

- What is their track record, what personal experience do they have?

Hands–Free Property Investment

There will be many of you who, having read this book, are keen to invest in Property but do not live locally to housing stock which meets the ideal price range (£55,000 – £100,000) and falls within the Gross Rental Yields we have identified. If this is the case you may wish to consider working with a Hands–Free Property Investment business, such as Alton Property Partners.

Hands–Free Investment Companies offer a fantastic solution if you, like David, are a busy professional or a Business Owner and you do not have the time (or inclination) to dedicate and commit to investing yourself. Hands–free investment companies are located across the whole of the UK and certainly most large cities will be serviced by at least one. So there is likely to be a company covering the area in which you wish to invest and you can employ their skills, knowledge, expertise and connections to fast track your investing.

However, before you start working with a Company are they prepared to spend time with you upfront to understand your personal goals? This is important as I know from my clients that everyone's circumstances are slightly different. 'One size' certainly does not fit all regarding your Pension Plan.

To help you select your Hands–Free Property Investing partner there are a number of elements I recommend you consider carefully. These are in no particular order, all are equally important:

- Which area of the UK do they specialise in? I would suggest it's better to work with different companies specialising in different areas, rather than one company who covers multiple areas, as their knowledge may be spread too thinly.

- When you met with them did they make you feel comfortable and importantly did you like them? (This human element is key, as you need to be able to work together effectively, particularly if untoward issues arise while investing).

- Do they, or have they invested themselves in the area they are promoting?

- Do you understand how they will produce their financial analysis and particularly 'what is and isn't' included in their calculations. I have seen a multitude of ways of sharing financial data and you need to ensure you are truly comparing 'apples with apples' Look at the diagram on the next page, this demonstrates how the same investment can be shown in 6 different ways. There is a very big difference between a cash–flow of £500 and that of £180 per month, so it's important that you do thorough financial due diligence when assessing cash–flow performance. It is easy to be misled.

    Remember all the costs we included in our calculations, how many of these do they allow for? Remember Gross Rental Yield is a great yardstick to compare one property against another but it's actually understanding and allowing for all the other costs which can make or break a deal.

- Do they have an existing refurbishment team and connections with Letting Agents?

- How are they proposing to bill you? As they purchase the properties, or upfront? If it's upfront what level of financial commitment are they looking for?

- If you are proposing to work with a Property Portfolio Building Company (remember this is a version of a Hands–Free investment business who promise to buy you a certain number of houses within a certain time frame, for an agreed sum of money upfront) and the required upfront payment is of considerable value i.e. £50k – £70k will your money be held in an escrow account? This is important as an escrow account protects your money against bankruptcy or insolvency. Can you have access to that account?

- Does the company have Professional Indemnity cover in case of losses due to bad advice?

Figure 62

Cash–Flow Analysis –Which Option is being quoted?

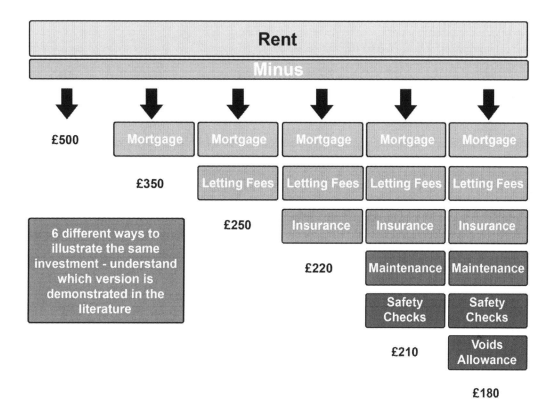

- In addition, can they confirm that they are a member of The Property Ombudsman? This will provide you with additional protection and the organisation will consider and resolve complaints against Member Agents. This can be very helpful should you get into a dispute.

- If you choose to work with a Portfolio Building Company what exit strategies are there within the contract should your circumstances change? Also what recourse do you have if they don't meet their commitments?

- If you commit to a Portfolio Building Company what financial contingency do you have to cover any additional costs which might occur along the way (e.g. to prevent your investment plan from getting 'stuck')?

- Whether you are purchasing through a Hands–free business or a Portfolio Builder what percentage of the property will you own on Day 1? If this is anything less than 100%, when will you be able to gain 100% ownership and what actions will you need to take to make this happen? A projection of your financial commitment at that time should be included in the initial financial analysis. Once you have a good idea of the funds you will require, what are your plans for sourcing that money to gain full title ownership or your properties?

- If you're not 100% owner from Day 1, what exit strategies do you have should your circumstances change and you need to sell?

- If you are planning to purchase via the Interest Only route what plans do you have for paying down the Debt on retirement?

In summary, utilising the skills, knowledge and connections of a company you trust can definitely be a sensible option when investing in property if you are a busy professional. They can deliver you 'peace of mind', and the pension income you desire, as long as you consider your debt repayment strategy as part of your Retirement Planning.

Finally, if you opt for help with investing you don't need to worry that the cost will negatively impact the financial illustrations in this book, as £5,000 per property has already been included in our figures.

29. Property Investment Pitfalls to Avoid!

Throughout this book I have sought to provide a balanced review of property investment, so if, like David, you are faced with a significant pension shortfall you can confidently take the necessary action to resolve your situation.

We have learnt that not all property investment is the same and;

'one size does not fit all'

… in terms of a Property Pension Strategy. The focus of this Chapter is therefore to highlight key pitfalls you should avoid – as they could cost you dearly.

i.   Letting agents

Avoid engaging a Letting Agent who is not local to your properties. We have allowed for 95% occupancy (based on a UK average of three weeks' void between tenants and the average UK tenancy of 20 months) in our calculations but this can easily extend if your agent isn't local, and is unable to act quickly to show prospective tenants around your property. Likewise they need to be able to resolve all maintenance issues in a timely manner.

Ensure your Letting Agent has sound processes and procedures established, so that money due to you can be paid quickly and efficiently, after all it is your Pension income. Ensure your Letting Agent provides documented regular inspections of your property.

ii.   Off Plan investments

At no point during this book when referring to 'investing in Property' have I meant "Off Plan" property i.e. property which has not yet been built.

This is your retirement planning strategy and we are focusing on cash flow, (with long term capital growth as a bonus). Purchasing 'Off Plan' is based 100% on gambling on capital growth and so is completely mis–aligned with the cash–flow strategy we have discussed in this book. Our 'Property investment' means investing in a physical property you can see, touch and feel, rather than being 100% reliant on the gloss of the marketing material.

With an Off Plan investment you wouldn't start receiving any rental income until the property is built, years in the future. And often when built the projected rental fails to live up to the overzealous projections, so the gross rental yield is not as expected.

Also from a practical viewpoint because you will not start to pay down your mortgage until the property is built, your mortgage could easily stretch far into your retirement years. As we have already discussed 'time' is not necessarily on your side, so you don't want to lose precious years.

I know the pain of buying 'Off Plan'. In the early 2000's my husband and I were attracted by the glossy marketing brochures and big promises, and naively purchased a city centre flat in Manchester.

In 2008 the developers went bankrupt, having been carried away with the rising market and failing to recognise the cyclical nature of the housing market. Their assumption that the prices of the properties would always be substantially higher on completion was flawed. When the market dropped investors had to complete on property which was instantly in negative equity, or worse still had not been built.

We were one of the fortunate ones, our flat had been built so even though it never attained the predicted value and the rent never achieved the promised level we did not lose our seed capital. Others however were less fortunate and, reports suggest, incurred losses between £50,000 and £500,000.

Looking back, our mistake was obvious, we had become complacent and had not done our due diligence. We had foolishly hung all our hopes on Capital Growth.

Thankfully, we learnt our lesson. A couple of years later we avoided another disaster with a Portfolio Building Company by taking the time to do our due diligence and discovered, with the help of a Lawyer friend, that the contract was totally biased in their favour. We walked away but many investors lost money when subsequently that company also went bankrupt.

So what can we learn from this?

Successful Property investment for your Pension involves due diligence, due diligence, due diligence. You need to be investing into a physical asset which you can assess fully, and which has the potential to bring you cash flow from Day 1.

I would recommend that you don't hand large sums of money over upfront; a small commitment fee is one thing but anything more can leave you exposed and certainly DO NOT BUY Off Plan.

iii.   Overseas investments

I would also advise heavily against investing in overseas properties, as this is fraught with danger.

Remember, our aim is to provide you with a steady rental income for your retirement years, but this is nigh on impossible to guarantee in a country you know little about. Throughout this book we have sought to provide a solution which gives you more control over your future, but currency fluctuations represent a huge risk for overseas investments.

You only need to look at the glut of Spanish properties following over expansion in the early 2000's, the subsequent financial crash and the ongoing Euro zone crisis and you will understand that many people, who were attracted by the glamour of 'owning a property abroad' are now holding a property they can't rent or sell. For them the glamour has turned into a living nightmare.

In fact, as I write this book another Overseas Property Investment Company is being scrutinized by the Serious Fraud Squad. Its UK Sales arm having recently gone into administration and the Directors have had their personal assets frozen.

In due course I'm sure we will learn the real truth behind the situation, but this will do little to appease the 3,000 British investors who potentially stand to lose their savings. Once again high yields, and capital growth presented in glossy brochures with celebrity endorsements, was too attractive to resist.

In this case, the situation is further exacerbated by the fact that many of these investments were made through a SIPP (Self Invested Pension Plan). However this scheme was not an FCA (aka FSA) regulated scheme, so if the scheme fails those who have invested stand to receive no compensation.
If they had understood what you now know, they would have recognised the lethal three way concoction they were entrusting their money too. Figure 63 below illustrates the point.

Figure 63

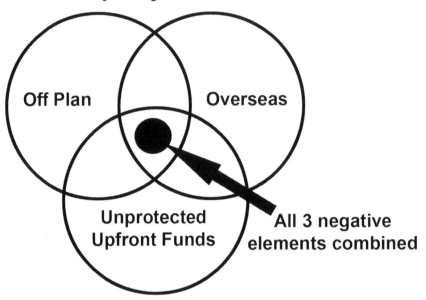

Lethal Concoction
for Property Investment

Off Plan

Overseas

Unprotected
Upfront Funds

All 3 negative
elements combined

iv.   **Property Investment Strategies where you don't gain Ownership.**

As an investor who is looking to increase your retirement income, there are several different strategies that could appear attractive. So why have I recommended only one strategy – 'Buy, Refurbish and Hold'?

The answer to this is based on your time–frame till retirement; you need to start with your end goal in mind. Your goal is to fill your pension shortfall with a reliable source of income, which provides you with peace of mind in your later years.

'Control' and 'ownership' are therefore essential elements of the journey you need to follow over the next 16 year period. Your aim is to build a small portfolio of unencumbered properties, and to outsource the management of these to a Letting Agent. This will not only ensure your retirement income is ring–fenced and protected from movement in the housing market, or changes in Government / Lending policies, but it will also mean your day to day involvement can be limited if you so choose.

My personal viewpoint is that other cash–flow investment strategies are more appropriate for different periods in an investor's life. For example, if you were starting to invest in property at age 21 you would have time on your side, so the requirement for ownership and full control is not so pressing. Likewise in your younger years it's likely you wouldn't mind having far more physical involvement in generating your cash–flow e.g. dashing around organizing refurbishments, arranging tenants, marketing your property etc.

In summary, each investment strategy offers its own merits, but choosing the wrong strategy at the wrong time in your life, would be like be trying to eat soup with a fork – time consuming, frustrating and pointless.

So my recommendation for your Retirement Rescue Plan is that you avoid any investment strategy which precludes you from 100% ownership of your property, or has increased risks associated with ownership and control over a prolonged period (as you do not have that time). I do not plan to go into each of these here, but they include strategies such as Lease Options, Instalment Contracts, Delayed Completion Contracts, Adverse Possession and Rent to Rent.

v.   Pension Liberation Schemes

Pension Liberation Schemes promise to give you access to your Pension Funds prior to you reaching age 55. This may seem tempting if you are looking to raise the capital to invest in property, and you are disillusioned with your pension fund. However, DO NOT be tempted, as these companies are currently being reviewed by the industry as fraudulent.

In terms of the fees it is likely the liberating company will be looking for a fee of around 15% of your fund value, to cover their work. This on its own doesn't sound too extortionate, however it is likely they will fail to inform you that you will also be liable for a tax bill based on 55% of the total value of the liberated pension savings, irrespective of your personal tax band.

Together these costs can wipe out nearly 85% of your fund, leaving you with very little. The stress for you may be even greater if, by the time you receive your Tax Bill, you have already spent your fund on a property and are then forced to remortgage or sell to pay the Tax man. A situation which should be avoided completely.

vi.   Lifetime Mortgage

Before finishing this Chapter of pitfalls I would also like to discuss Lifetime Mortgages. This is a type of Equity Release but it is completely different from the strategy which has been covered in this book, so please ensure you do not get the two confused.

A Lifetime Mortgage involves deliberately taking debt into your retirement, so is a fundamentally different strategy. The Debt and interest on the money released from your home is not due to be repaid until such time as you pass away or sell the house. As the interest is 'rolled up' to the end of the term it can be a classic example of the power of compounding working against you, as a relatively modest release of equity can overtime add up to a substantial amount, which must be paid from the estate of the deceased.

Because of the significant impact on the remaining family members, specialist Mortgage Brokers are required to sell this product, to ensure the client understands the implications. The client is also encouraged to inform their family of their decision.

In most cases the outstanding debt has to be repaid to the lender within a given time frame e.g. six months. This may involve a lot of negotiations on behalf of the Executors, and the beneficiaries of the Will may be forced to take out a loan if the sale of the property cannot be completed in time.

This was the exact situation faced by the family of an ex–work colleague. The original equity release of £20,000 rose in value to £55,000 which had to be repaid at a time when the housing market was stagnant and it was difficult to sell the property.

So to clarify, when I talk about releasing equity I do not mean via a Lifetime Mortgage.

Now that you have read this book you will understand that wise Property investment for your retirement is a 'fact based investment decision'. It is not based on fiction. It's about 'cash–flow' and cash–flow is only achieved when you have a physical asset in front of you, bought with full due diligence. It's about investing with care and knowledge and not being attracted by any promises of overnight success. It's about gaining control and not taking debt into your retirement.

We have proven, with David, that wise Property investment has the power to deliver your Retirement Rescue Plan but it takes time, patience and consideration. Simply do not be tempted to cut corners.

Finally, remember there is always movement in the property market, capital growth figures and returns can be projected but NEVER guaranteed. **Property is not a 'get rich overnight scheme'.** Success for retirement is based on playing the long game with a property which is a physical tangible asset.

The saying; *'If it's too good to be true, it probably is'* holds as reliably in the Property investment world, as it does elsewhere.

Section
Four

Your Step–by–Step
Retirement Rescue Plan

30. Your 15 Step Retirement Rescue Plan

Now that you understand how wise Property investment can allow you to address your Pension Shortfall, this Chapter brings together all the elements we have discussed, so that you can establish you own personal 'Retirement Rescue Plan'.

Having a Plan is a critical step to success as it provides a structure from which to work and helps convert all the ideas discussed into actions.

Step 1 – Calculate your Pension Shortfall.

This is the most important step, because unless you shock yourself with the size of your Pension Shortfall you are unlikely to take the action that is needed.

There are a multitude of websites which will help you gain an overview of your pension outlook. However, as a word of warning, every site I visited provided a slightly different answer. You also need to ensure they are producing a projection based on a 5% compound growth rate (remember the current default setting on most websites is misleading if it is still set at 7% pa) and include any relevant inflationary or fixed increases.

Finally, if you are planning to provide a pension for your spouse on your death, you will need to ensure you specify this for your online calculations. This may involve going into 'Advanced Options', or a similarly named button, to override the standard criteria.

An alternative and more accurate reflection of your Pension shortfall, however, may be achieved by referring to your latest Annual Pension Statement.

Figure 64, on page 215 is an example of how to read your Pension Statement, taken from www.moneyvista.com. (You will note in the assumptions in this example the fund growth rate is already set at 5% per annum. Also the illustrated pension will increase annually by inflation, and is for a single life only).

Following, are the notes taken from the moneyvista.com website which explain the numbers on the Statement.

Notes from website:

1. In this case, the pension year is the anniversary of starting the scheme.
2. The value of your pension fund at the end of the year taking into account payments in, investment growth added and charges deducted.
3. The amount available if you transferred your savings to another provider's scheme. It will be less than the value of the pension fund if some charges would be deducted.
4. For comparison, the transfer value of your pension fund at the start of the year.
5. Contributions made by your employer, in this example £75 a month (for example, as part of a group personal pension scheme arrangement).
6. The age at which you have said you want your pension income to start.
7. The amount of pension income you might get. It is in today's money. This means that, although at age 66 you would get a larger amount in pounds, the buying power of the pension would be the same as £3,580 today. This figure assumes you use the whole fund to provide a pension. If you take part of the fund as a tax–free lump sum (also called a pension commencement lump sum or PCLS) the pension will be lower.
8. The estimated pension income of £3,580 is based on the assumptions explained here. If, say, investment returns or annuity rates were lower, you would get less. Conversely, if they were higher, you would get more.
9. Details about the charges deducted.
10. Tax relief at the basic rate on the contributions paid by you.
11. The amount of contributions you have paid in over the year – in this case, £100 a month.

Figure 64

Example of a Personal Pension Statement

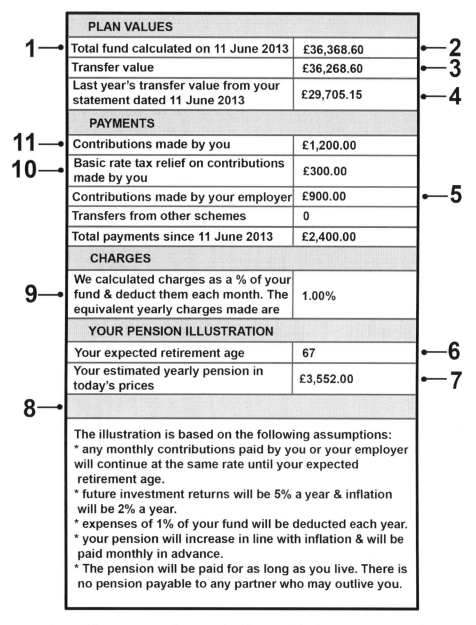

1 → PLAN VALUES

Total fund calculated on 11 June 2013	£36,368.60
Transfer value	£36,268.60
Last year's transfer value from your statement dated 11 June 2013	£29,705.15

PAYMENTS

Contributions made by you	£1,200.00
Basic rate tax relief on contributions made by you	£300.00
Contributions made by your employer	£900.00
Transfers from other schemes	0
Total payments since 11 June 2013	£2,400.00

CHARGES

We calculated charges as a % of your fund & deduct them each month. The equivalent yearly charges made are	1.00%

YOUR PENSION ILLUSTRATION

Your expected retirement age	67
Your estimated yearly pension in today's prices	£3,552.00

The illustration is based on the following assumptions:
* any monthly contributions paid by you or your employer will continue at the same rate until your expected retirement age.
* future investment returns will be 5% a year & inflation will be 2% a year.
* expenses of 1% of your fund will be deducted each year.
* your pension will increase in line with inflation & will be paid monthly in advance.
* The pension will be paid for as long as you live. There is no pension payable to any partner who may outlive you.

Source: https://www.moneyvista.com/guides–tools/retirement–pensions/understanding– your pension statement/

On your Pension Statement it is critical you check the growth rate used is 5% pa and not 7%, as it is this reduction in growth which will dramatically increase your Pension Shortfall. If your statement is still being calculated at 7% pa I would recommend you follow the steps below to give you a more accurate picture of how your Pension is performing.

How to re–calculate your Pension Fund based on 5% Compound Growth rate.

To re–calculate your Pension Fund based on 5% compound growth, please follow the steps detailed below:

1. **Calculate the size of the Fund the current illustration is projecting**

   - To do this, you will need to understand the annuity rate that has been used in the illustration. If there is no annuity rate quoted, then refer to the notes to decipher the annuity terms which have been adopted. e.g. in the example in Figure 64 the annuity terms are based on 'Single Life, Retail Price Indexed (RPI)'

   - Search the internet for a competitive annuity rate which meets the terms used in the calculations. Let's assume in this case a Single Life, RPI rate is £3,545 per £100,000 of Pension Fund.

   - Take your Projected 'Estimated Yearly Pension in Today's Prices' and divide it by the annuity rate i.e. 3,545, and multiply by 100,000.

   - In the example the Estimated Yearly Pension in Today's prices shown on the statement is £3,552. Therefore, the estimated Fund Value at retirement is:

   $$\frac{3{,}552 \times 100{,}000}{3{,}545} = £100{,}197$$

2. **Convert this Fund to more accurately reflect reality**

   - From the table overleaf select the number of years you have before retirement and apply the appropriate percentage to your estimated Fund Value.

- For example, if you are due to retire in 16 years your projected Pension Fund value of £100,197 would reduce to £74,046 based on a 5% compound growth rate per annum.

  i.e. £100,197 x 73.9% = £74,046

  This is a reduction of 26.1%!

Figure 65

Re–adjusting 7% Compound Growth Rate to 5% Compound Growth Rate					
Number of years Till Retirement	Multiply Fund Size by	Number of years Till Retirement	Multiply Fund Size by	Number of years Till Retirement	Multiply Fund Size by
1	98.1%	11	81.3%	21	67.3%
2	96.3%	12	79.7%	22	66.0%
3	94.5%	13	78.2%	23	64.8%
4	92.7%	14	76.8%	24	63.6%
5	91.0%	15	75.3%	25	62.4%
6	89.3%	16	73.9%		
7	87.6%	17	72.6%		
8	86.0%	18	71.2%		
9	84.4%	19	69.9%		
10	82.8%	20	68.6%		

3. **Calculate your projected Pension based on this new Fund value**

- Apply the annuity rate of £3,545 per £100,000 to your revised Fund value

$$\frac{74,046 \times 3,545}{100,000} = £2,625$$

Your estimated yearly pension is now £2625 (£927 per annum less than previously thought!)

How to Calculate Your Projected Pension Shortfall

Now that you have calculated the size of your pension **(A)** (based on your continuing with your existing arrangements and 5% compound growth) you need to add your State Pension **(B)** to obtain a realistic illustration of your total income in retirement. (You may choose to ignore the State Pension if you feel strongly that this will no longer exist by the time you retire).

Figure 66

Total Projected Income in Retirement		
Projected Pension Income @ 5% Compound Growth pa	A	£
State Pension (based on £144 per week)	B	£7,488
Total Projected Income in Retirement (A + B)	**C**	£

Calculate the Income you require in Retirement.

The income you require in retirement is likely to be less than you currently need. 70% of your pre–retirement income is a frequently quoted rule of thumb. However, this is making the assumption that you are debt free as you enter retirement. In the current economic climate there is a school of thought that 80% of pre–retirement income would be a more accurate figure.

Of course, the best approximation would be achieved by carefully reviewing your budget and understanding your exact spend.

However, for the purposes of getting yourself started you may wish to adopt the 80% rule. This means taking your current net income and multiplying it by 80%, which will give you an indication of the income you will require in retirement. See the table on the next page, which allows for two salaries.

Figure 67

Income Requirement in Retirement		
Net Salary Person 1	D	£
Net Salary Person 2	E	£
Total Current Net Income	**F**	**£**

Income Requirement in Retirement (F x 80%)	**G**	**£**

To calculate your Pension Shortfall:

Now that you have established your income requirement in retirement and a projection of your current pension outlook, simply take one from the other to establish the size of your Pension Shortfall.

Figure 68

Your Pension Shortfall		
Income Requirement in Retirement	G	£
Total Projected Income in Retirement	C	£
Your Pension Shortfall (G – C)	**H**	**£**

Before you panic, follow the remaining steps of your Retirement Rescue Plan.

Note: These tables can be downloaded at www.gillalton.com

Step 2 – Establish your capital for Investment

Having made the decision to utilise Property as a Retirement Rescue Plan, you need to calculate the amount of investment money you have available. The tables over the next few pages are downloadable as one document, at www.gillalton.com, I would suggest you save it and add your personal details.

As a worked example, I have completed the form for David and if this looks rather daunting, don't panic, clear instructions follow the tables.

Figure 69

TO CALCULATE POTENTIAL CAPITAL FOR INVESTING

1 – SAVINGS			
Account Name	**Access**	**Account No.**	**Savings £**
Nationwide	Instant	12358989	£8,000
Halifax Savings	3 months	54689712	£3,000
Santander	2 months	123458963	£3,000
Post Office	Instant	123489321	£7,000
TOTAL SAVINGS			£21,000
TOTAL AMOUNT HAPPY TO COMMIT TO RESCUE PLAN (A)			£12,600

2 – CURRENT MORTGAGE POTENTIAL OF YOUR HOME	
	Value £
Current Value of Your Home **(B)**	£380,000
75% of Current Value **(C)**	£285,000

3 –MORTGAGE DEBT		
Existing Mortgage / Second Charges		
Lender	Interest Rate	Mortgage Amount
Barclays Bank	4.75%	£45,000
TOTAL MORTGAGE DEBT (D)		£45,000
Are you within an Early Redemption Period?		Yes / **No**
POTENTIAL MONEY AVAILABLE FOR INVESTING (C – D) (E)		£240,000

4 – CREDIT CARD AND LOAN DEBT			
Credit Cards	Outstanding Balance £	3% of Balance	Annual Commitment (3% of Balance x 12)
Mastercard	£1,500	£45	£540
Visa	£900	£27	£324
Loans	Outstanding Balance £	Monthly Payment	Annual Commitment (12 x Mthly Payment)
Car	£4,500	£275	£3,300
TOTAL ANNUAL CREDIT / LOAN COMMITMENT (F)			£4,164

5 – GROSS INCOME		
	Name	Gross Income £
1	David	£42,780
2	David's Wife	£12,000
TOTAL HOUSEHOLD INCOME **(H)**		£54,780
MINUS CURRENT ANNUAL CREDIT / LOAN COMMITMENT (F)		£4,164
INCOME AVAILABLE (H – F) **(G)**		£50,616

6 – MORTGAGE CAPACITY (Complete Either No. 1 or No. 2)		
1	Sole Income Multiply (G) by 4.25 **(I)**	
2	Joint Income Multiply (G) by 4 **(I)**	£202,464

7 – CURRENTLY UNUSED MORTGAGE CAPACITY	
Potential Money available (I – D) = **(J)**	£157,464

8 – MONEY AVAILABLE TO RELEASE THROUGH RE–MORTGAGE	
The lower value between (E) OR (J) = **(K)**	£157,464

9 – TOTAL MONEY AVAILABLE FOR RESCUE PLAN	
Item	Value £
Savings **(A)**	£12,600
Equity Release **(K)**	£157,464
TOTAL INVESTMENT FOR RESCUE PLAN	**£170,064**

Instructions on how to complete the document.

1. Savings

David has four savings accounts. I have deliberately left space for several saving accounts, as you may have money spread across many different pots. Including all your savings pots may provide you with more than you had originally anticipated.

Remember utilising savings for investment will be considerably cheaper than the costs we have put in our calculations, so the savings on offer will be even greater.

When you are completing this information try to note how quickly you can get access to your savings e.g. 30 days, 90 days etc., as this will remind you how much notice you need to give, to avoid penalties.

Then determine how much of your total savings you wish to commit to your Retirement Rescue Plan. In David's example I have kept 40% of his savings back. I would recommend you **must** always keep some money back for a 'rainy day', do not spend your last penny. Enter the figure you are happy to commit in box **(A)**.

Bonus

As an added bonus and to help you boost your savings you may also wish to download from www.gillalton.com my Budget Planning Documents. Knowing exactly where your money is currently being spent, and what your financial priorities are, can have a dramatic effect on your ability to save – and you may well amaze yourself to find minor changes can produce major benefits.

One of my mentees who has committed to this process has instantly realised a few key / quick wins and has been able to save a staggering £500 per month. If budgeting is not part of your current household routine, I would encourage you to embrace it as it's a great discipline.

2. Current Mortgage Potential of Your Home

The need to source additional monies by releasing equity from you home (which you pay back before retirement) will be based on the difference between the savings you have, and are happy to spend, and the desired 'Total Equity' requirement.

You can calculate the potential value in your home that you could access by completing the form you have downloaded as follows:

i. Document the current value of your home, **(B)**. Be realistic with your figure; as there is no point in trying to fool yourself.

ii. Calculate 75% of this value to indicate the remortgage value your home could support **(C)**. (I have deliberately selected 75% as I like to work with a buffer, but you may wish to take this higher or lower i.e. 80% or 60%). Remember this remortgaged capital MUST be repaid on a Repayment basis, as we do not want you to take debt into your retirement.

3. Mortgage Debt

Record the value of your existing mortgage and any other debts already secured on your home and put the total in box **(D)**. How much money you have available to invest will be influenced by your existing debts.

Check whether you are within any Early Redemption Period on your existing mortgage. If you are you will need to ensure your Independent Mortgage Broker is aware of this, so you can work with him to minimise any financial penalties.

Establish the potential equity available for investing **(E)**, by deducting your Total Debt **(D)** from the current mortgage potential on your home **(C)**.

4. Credit Card and Loan Debt

Understand that the potential mortgage capacity based on house value alone is only one side of the equation. Ultimately, the Bank will determine how much it is happy to lend you based on your income(s) and you existing financial commitments.

i. Complete your Credit Card details. Document any existing outstanding balance. Then calculate 3% of this balance and enter it into the box. Once you have calculated this figure multiple it by 12 so that you can capture your Annual Commitment.

ii. Complete any Loan details. Document the existing balance and the monthly payments you make. Multiple the monthly payments by 12 to calculate your Annual Commitment.

iii. Enter the total Annual Commitment, adding the Credit Card and Loan commitments together and putting in box **(F)**.

5. Gross Income

   i.   As we know David earns £42,780. His wife earns £12,000. Enter your gross incomes into the boxes and add up your total household income, capture this in box **(H)**.

   ii.   The bank will only lend based on your gross income after you have accounted for any existing financial commitments. So copy your Annual Financial Commitment figure across from box **(F)**.

   iii.   Deduct the Annual Financial Commitment **(F)** from the gross household income **(H)** and enter the answer into box **(G)**.

6. Mortgage Capacity

   i.   In the example I have completed row 2 as we have taken into consideration both David and his wife's Gross Incomes. If you are the sole owner of your home please complete row 1.

   ii.   Complete the appropriate row by taking your answer from box (G) and multiplying by the relevant figures (i.e. 4.25 or 4). Enter your answer into box **(I)**. **Note:** At this stage these are just multiplier guides, as banks will lend differently based on personal circumstances. Generally speaking the higher the incomes, the greater the multiplier they are happy to apply.

7. Currently Unused Mortgage Capacity

   i.   To calculate the potential money you are able to access for investment purposes deduct your current Mortgage Debt **(D)** from your Mortgage Capacity **(I)**. Enter your answer into box **(J)**.

8. Mortgage Money Available to Release

   i.   Being able to calculate your unused mortgage capacity is the start for understanding how much equity you have available to work with for investment purposes, as you can only release that money which the bank perceives you are able to pay back.

ii. To calculate the money the bank would be happy to lend to you, look at your answers in boxes (E) and (J). Whichever box is the lowest figure, enter into box **(J)**.

So:

If (E) is greater than (J) = (J)
If (J) is greater than (E) = (E)

In our example David has £240,000 of potential money available in his house for investing (E). However, based on the incomes coming into the household and his existing financial commitments he can only actually support a remortgage of £157,464 (J). This means the money he is able to release through his remortgage is this lower figure.

9. Total Money Available for Rescue Plan

Once you have confirmed the money able to be remortgaged out of your home, add this to the value of the Savings you are prepared to utilise for investment to calculate your Total investment pot:

- Savings: £ (A)
- Remortgage Equity: £ (K)
- **Total Investment Capital For Rescue Plan:** **£ A + K**

The figures you have calculated for yourself will provide a helpful guide, but I would always recommend you have them validated by your Mortgage Broker prior to starting your investment journey as Bank lending criteria are constantly changing, which could impact your funds.

Recommendations:

Keep a Financial Buffer: As a reminder never spend to your last penny. Even if you put money aside each month for maintenance as suggested, I guarantee your property costs will not arrive in conveniently sized monthly portions. A financial buffer will also provide tremendous peace of mind, as remember your home is at risk if you do not keep up repayments on a mortgage secured on it.

Protect your Credit Rating: Although lending criteria is a moving target, some elements remain constant. For example the need to be able to prove a sound Credit

Rating before the Bank will lend to you has been imperative since the Financial Crash of 2008.

There are three Credit Agencies in the UK, Experian, Equifax and CallCredit they all have slightly different criteria, but their results will be similar, so if you don't already know your Credit Score I would recommend you find it out by going to **www.checkmyfile.com**. This is a consumer credit site and pulls information from all three agencies. You will need to complete your Personal Profile.

From our family Mortgage Business, Alton Mortgages Ltd www.altonmortgages.co.uk my husband has experienced occasions where clients are totally unaware that there is a mark on their file for a missed or late payment. In addition, sometimes there are errors on Reports, which will affect your ability to raise capital. By pulling off your Report, for a small fee, you can gain an understanding of how the Banks are viewing you as a credit risk. The question is would you lend money to yourself based on your score?

If you have decided that investing in Property is going to be your Retirement Rescue Plan then it is imperative that you maintain a strong credit score. Below are some tips to help you achieve this:

i. Make sure all your bill payments are set up on **Direct Debit**, which at least covers the minimum payment due. Ensure you include Council Tax Bills, Utility Bills, Mobile Phone Bills, Credit Cards and Store Cards. Unfortunately it is notoriously easy to gain a 'late payment', if you shop online with any catalogue company so use Direct Debit to safeguard your credit score.

ii. Ensure you are on the **Electoral Roll** at your current residence as this shows stability to the Bank and gains additional points on your score.

iii. Include your **home telephone number** when you complete any forms – this indicates more stability than a mobile phone number.

iv. **Never take out a Pay Day Loan** – to a Bank this suggests that you are unable to manage your money and will prevent you from getting any mortgages.

v. Make sure you **DO HAVE a credit card** (or two) and pay it off in full each month. Banks want to see you can handle money responsibly, having no credit cards is actually a disadvantage, as they have no history on which to base their assessment of you.

vi. **Do not have an online Gambling Account** as this can affect lending decisions (not specifically your Credit Score).

vii.   Look at the **aliases** on your Credit Profile and 'dissociate' yourself financially from anyone with whom you have no financial commitment as their Credit Score may affect you.

viii.   **Stability of employment** is also attractive to a lender, so think twice about constantly changing companies if you hope to release equity.

Step 3 – Understand Your Personal Risk Profile

Understanding your risk profile is imperative as it is likely to influence which mortgage route you plan to follow. Your risk profile will be very personal and based on your individual circumstances and how comfortable you are with handling uncertainty / risk.

I believe, whether you favour an Interest Only or Repayment Mortgage you should be guided by your ability to pay off the debt. Remember our aim is to ensure you enter retirement with unencumbered properties.

The diagram below may help you clarify your thoughts.

Figure 70

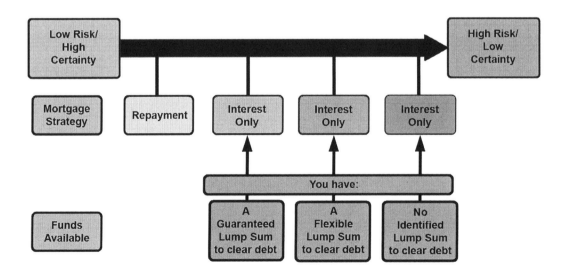

As we have discussed throughout this book, the Repayment option represents the greatest certainty. However, Interest Only can still be a viable option if you have a guaranteed future lump sum from an alternative source.

The less certain, or more risky, your future lump sum is in terms of value and timing, the greater the risk with purchasing via an Interest Only Mortgage.

Whichever strategy you choose if you are purchasing with a partner it is important you both understand and are jointly committed to driving the results.

Of course there is nothing to prevent you from creating your own personal hybrid solution, with a mixture of Repayment and Interest Only.

As a family we have created our own hybrid with our houses on Interest Only Mortgages being overpaid each month to the level of a Repayment Mortgage. Technically this means we are actively reducing our debt each and every month, just like a Repayment Mortgage, but we have also kept the flexibility to be able to react to unforeseen financial circumstances. We believe this solution provides us with the 'best of both worlds'.

Most mortgages allow you to overpay each year to the level of 10% of the outstanding mortgage debt – although check with your Mortgage Broker, so you are not hit with any early redemption fees.

To summarise, our personal preference is to overpay an Interest–Only Mortgage because it offers the key advantage of a greater degree of flexibility for emergencies. For example, if a large maintenance bill should arise or we are off work due to sickness, one call to the Bank and we are able to reduce our monthly payment back to the Interest Only level. Never being in arrears at the Bank is of paramount importance.

I would, however, only recommend this approach if you are disciplined enough to maintain the overpayments (only dipping into them for 'real investment emergencies'). Otherwise you will only be fooling yourself and you will still have a significant debt overhang at retirement.

And remember if you're able to overpay the Repayment Mortgage level, even by a small amount each month it can have a dramatic effect on reducing your mortgage term and the total amount of interest paid.

Look back at page 98 where we explained that by overpaying the repayment level by just 10% – which in this case was £36.50 per month, the mortgage term was reduced by 2 years and 4 months, saving £4,006 in interest payments).

Step 4 – Identify the price range you want to target

Based on your Investment Capital available (already calculated in Step 2) and your choice of mortgage type, identified in Step 3 you will now be able to establish an appropriate house price range. I suggest you select a range of prices because it is highly unlikely all your houses will be exactly the same price.

Your price range will impact the location you select in Step 5.

Note: Remember the lower the price range the greater the probability of attracting tenants who receive Housing Benefit. Moving up the price range will increase your chances of securing a private tenant.

Step 5 – Identify Your Investing Area

Identifying your area is easy if it is right on your doorstep, but more challenging if you don't live where you wish to buy your houses.

If you aim to invest locally, to help you identify an area draw concentric circles on a map radiating out from your home. As your circles radiate out and incorporate new areas review them on www.rightmove.co.uk and ascertain the size of housing stock within the price band you have selected in Step 4.

Remember you don't want to be looking to source houses in a location where there is minimal stock – this will not only make your job extremely difficult but importantly it could also impact rental demand.

Utilise the internet i.e. www.rightmove.co.uk and www.zoopla.co.uk to ascertain the average rental values for each locality. If you're planning to invest in an area where there is a high probability that families will be in receipt of Housing Benefit go to the following link to calculate their payment entitlement:

www.lha–direct.voa.gov.uk/search.aspx.

And finally, remember the following Gross Rental Yield equation:

$$\text{Gross Rental Yield} = \frac{\text{Annual Rental Income}}{\text{Purchase Price}}$$

There are certainly advantages in keeping your investing area as close as possible, but of course if you have an existing connection with a location further afield e.g. it's where you were brought up, you may wish to utilise your knowledge/relationship and select this as your investment area.

Wherever your location the key to success is the same:

- Know your area
- Focus and commit time
- Build relationships

If this all sounds too much, as your life is already jammed packed with commitments, or you simply don't have the desire to become personally involved, I would recommend you leverage the skills, time and knowledge of a Hands–Free Investing Company. Selecting this option makes the location less critical but it would still be preferable if your houses are close enough to facilitate viewing visits without having to include an overnight stay. For this, together with all the reasons given in Chapter 29, make sure you stay within the UK.

Step 6 – Educate yourself or Evaluate and Select your Hands–Free Investment Partner

Whichever route you choose I would recommend you re–read Chapter 28 and carefully go through each question to ensure you go into your relationship with your eyes open. There is no right or wrong way to invest, it's what works for you.

If you choose to invest for yourself be mindful of managing the fine line between being guilty of cutting educational corners and becoming a "course junkie". Remember true success comes to those who not only plan and take action, but also constantly review where they could make improvements.

Step 7 – Build your team

If you have decided to invest for yourself you need to consider building your team, so when an investment opportunity arises you can act quickly and decisively. As a guide you will most definitely require the following professionals in your team, so the sooner you start building relationships the better:

Estate Agents: I would recommend you work with two or three key Estate Agents in your chosen location. Attend viewings and explain your criteria (but do not talk about Gross Rental Yields, it only confuses). Also don't be tempted to put out numerous offers that you have no intention of following through. Remember Estate Agents are no different from you and I and can easily get fed up with people they consider to be time wasters. My advice is to be factual, polite, thoughtful and realistic with your Estate Agents (e.g. give them proactive feedback if a property does not meet your requirements, as it helps educate them regarding your criteria). And most importantly follow through on what you say you will do.

Never forget a good Estate Agent in your team is a real asset.

Mortgage Broker: We have already mentioned the Mortgage Broker in Step 2. It's essential you work with an Independent Broker (i.e. 'whole of market) as no High Street Bank has access to all the Buy–to–Let mortgage products and you will waste valuable time going from Bank to Bank. Being able to view the whole market means your Independent Broker can truly offer you the best product in a timely manner to meet your personal requirements.

Your Broker will also be able to source the most comprehensive Landlord Insurance. As we have talked throughout this book about reducing your risk, having the right Insurance is essential and standard High Street products will leave you financially exposed.

The relationship with your Mortgage Broker is additionally important as they are able to arrange both the Buy–To–Let Mortgage and the Remortgage of your home to raise your equity.

Solicitor: Identify a couple of Solicitors you would be comfortable to work with, as this will give you options when the time comes. In addition, utilising a Solicitor from the Bank's panel means you may be able to achieve a more competitive interest rate or Arrangement Fee, so it is definitely worth considering. If you're buying Repossessions I would recommend you confirm that your Solicitor has experience in this area and understands the speed with which they will need to work.

We have not discussed the Repossession process in this book per se, but suffice to say with Repossessions – 'speed is of the essence' as the property cannot be taken off the market until such time as an Exchange of Contracts has occurred.

Refurbishment Team: As you are probably planning to 'Add Value' to your property through a refurbishment it's worth identifying the key personnel upfront so you don't waste time later. You will need a Builder, Plumber, Electrician, Decorator and Carpenter. (You may find that the Builder is happy to project manage the whole process, which can make it considerably easier for you, but make sure you understand the costs involved).

If you are working with individual tradesmen, ideally meet with them before investing and understand their charging structure. This will allow you to plan who you should include in your team.

If you are new to the world of refurbishing, a sensible solution would be to get tradesman to view the property with you prior to making an offer, so you can cost out the refurbishment work together. Discussions with the Builder etc., before you purchase, can really help you ensure your investment remains a good deal even after the refurbishment. However if getting Builders on site, at the same time as yourself isn't feasible I suggest you provide them with a full Schedule of Works required, including if possible photos of the key areas. Ask them to allocate costs against each item (rather than just a Job Cost) to allow you to understand where savings may be made if necessary.

With a Schedule of Works you can also effectively compare one tradesman against another.

Finally, during the early stage of investing I would recommend you always work with a 15% contingency fund (You can fine tune this as you become more comfortable with the costs) and you should obtain three quotes – you'll be amazed at how much they vary. But remember the cheapest isn't always the best!

Letting Agent: do your homework and identify which Letting Agent you are going to engage. I would recommend you select them prior to purchasing, or at the latest between Exchange and Completion, to ensure they are promoting your property to prospective tenants from midway through the refurbishment. If you are planning to rent to tenants who receive Housing Benefit I would recommend your Letting Agent is based locally to the investment property, as your tenants many not have their own transport.

Step 8 – Start Buying and ensure you keep a Maintenance Buffer

From Step 2, you will now have a clear idea of the total capital you have available to invest, so you, or your Hands–Free Partner on your behalf, can start investing as soon as you have your savings ready and the process of releasing Equity from your home is underway (if you are combining sources). However don't forget to retain a buffer of money for emergencies.

Even if you follow my recommendation to save a percentage of your monthly rental income for maintenance, you will need to have a starting "emergency pot". Remember, maintenance issues rarely wait until your fund has conveniently built up.

Also I would recommend if you are buying with a partner you purchase the houses in individual names, as this protects your assets in 4 main ways:

i.   It allows you to purchase several houses in quick succession. Banks do not like to see several applications in the pipeline for the same person at any one time. Buying in alternate names allows you to get around this issue, as normally one Sale has completed before you need to buy another property. (Note: this is how my husband and I purchased 9 houses in very quick succession)

ii.   It allows you to maximise your lending capacity and leaves you open to be able to go after the most competitive mortgage deals. i.e. some banks have a limit of only 3 investment properties across their banking group. By buying in single names you are able to have three properties in your name with that lender and another three in your spouse / partner's name, therefore instantly doubling your mortgage capacity.

iii.   Finally, and not insignificantly. In the unfortunate event of a divorce if the houses are already in separate names it would remove the requirement to have them valued for purposes of splitting title. This is a major advantage as revaluing to split title automatically produces a Capital Gains Tax bill which will need to be paid as part of the divorce settlement. If the bill is large this may involve selling some of the properties.

Step 9 – Budget Monthly

Remember you need to budget monthly for property costs. So ensure you remain disciplined and throughout the term of the mortgage utilise your rental income to cover your property expenses. This allows you to leverage the income from your tenants to build your future retirement.

Failure to budget adequately is a sure–fire way to become despondent with your investment and start to feel it's not delivering on your retirement goals, even if it's performing as predicted.

From a maintenance viewpoint as a landlord it is your responsibility to keep your tenants (and their pets) safe, so you need to know you can act quickly to resolve any issues which arise. We have found the easiest way to budget monthly is to physically transfer the maintenance / insurance monies into a separate Bank Account. That way it can't be spent by mistake and we can monitor how big the pot has grown.

Step 10 – Work Closely with a Letting Agent

In Step 7 you identified which Agent(s) you wanted to work with, so now is the time to start working closely with them. Remember your investment only becomes an asset when it starts producing regular rental income. It's this rental income which is your pension. A close and strong working relationship with your Letting Agent is of fundamental importance, as they control your income flow.

Although you should consider your Letting Agent to be a valuable member of your team I recommend that you never abdicate responsibility completely.

Remember we are treating your properties as a business so would you leave an employee in charge indefinitely and expect to return to a smooth running, profitable organisation?

Working with your Letting Agent is a joint–venture and a relationship you need to continue to cultivate.

Step 11 –Appoint an Accountant and Change your Will

Your rental income is taxable. However, as we know there are tax allowances you can benefit from, so it is definitely worthwhile appointing an Accountant to ensure you maximise the opportunities available to you. The ideal solution is to appoint an Accountant who invests in property themselves, or already supports several other Property Investors, as this can ensure you receive proactive property tax advice.

Also if you don't have a Will you must write one and if you already have a Will I would recommend you update it, so it is relevant and includes your properties.

One of the key benefits of property is that unlike your pension, it won't die with you and it's your responsibility to ensure your properties are inherited by the people of your choice. This way, future generations can benefit from the sound investment strategy you have implemented.

Step 12 – Monitor the Housing Market and Capital Gains Tax

If Interest Only is your investment strategy during the term of your mortgage you should regularly monitor the Housing Market. Remember the Interest Only strategy is reliant on your property rising in value (unless you have an external income stream to pay off the debt).

Monitoring the market will allow you to recognize when the market fails to move in your favour. The more time you have to implement any necessary changes the better. This may include moving your portfolio onto Repayment Mortgages.

Likewise, if you adopt the Interest Only route I would also recommend you keep up–to–date with changes in the Capital Gains Tax rules, as these will impact your strategy. Reacting proactively is far better than feeling you have no control.

Step 13 – Clear Outstanding Debt

This Step is only required if you selected an Interest Only Strategy, as the Repayment Mortgage term will cease on the final mortgage payment. Clearing the outstanding debt on Interest Only properties, ready for your retirement, could involve selling some of your portfolio to release capital to clear debt.

If you have continued to pay into a Pension Scheme during the 16 year term, utilising your 25% Tax Free Lump Sum to clear debts may be an option. (Although remember there is no such thing as a 'free lunch' so this action will reduce the monthly income from your remaining pension pot).

You will need to ascertain which is the best route for you.

By this stage, if you have followed the Retirement Rescue Plan recommended in this book you should have a clear Action Plan and you are ready to hit the ground running.

Step 14 – Protect Your Property from Inheritance Tax

There are legal ways you can reduce the inheritance tax due on your properties. For example, you can transfer them into a Beneficiary Trust. If you were to live a further 7 years after the date of transfer there would be 0% inheritance tax to pay. So certainly, once your properties are unencumbered and pumping retirement income into your pocket each and every month, it is worth investigating how you can protect your family from having to pay an extortionate Inheritance Tax Bill on your death.

There are several books in this area which will give you an overview, however the best thing would be to speak to a specialist Tax Advisor.

Having worked hard to rescue your Retirement, how wonderful it will feel to know your family members will continue to benefit even after your passing.

Step 15 – Enjoy Your Retirement

Finally enjoy your properties and more importantly the opportunities the income brings you.

I wish for you the happy retirement you deserve.

Appendix

Annual Income		
Desired retirement income	24,500	
Less Income Tax	3,012	
Available to Spend		**£21,488**

Annual Expenditure		
Council Tax and Utilities		
Council Tax	1,517	
Gas	830	
Electricity	630	
Water & Sewerage	457	
Tel. & Broadband	350	
TV Licence	146	
House & Contents Insurance	310	4,240
Food and the Home		
Housekeeping	5,400	
Home	1,600	
Garden	700	7,700
Car Running Costs		
Car Insurance & Road Tax	460	
MOT & Servicing	240	
Petrol	600	1,300
Personal Expenditure		
Clothes & Personal Items	3,000	
Healthcare	800	3,800
Other Outgoings		
Leisure Activities	1,140	
Family Birthdays & Christmas	1,100	
Holidays	2,200	4,440
Total Spend		**£21,480**

About the Author

My journey into the world of property investing started 17 years ago.

Having left University in 1991 I ventured into the corporate world, enjoying a variety of Sales and Managerial roles. Property investment didn't appear on my radar until 1996 when my then boyfriend (now husband) bought his first investment property at the young age of 23. In fact, when we met he was living in what I now know to be a House of Multiple Occupation (HMO), having realised that he could earn more money by renting out his own home and living in cheaper accommodation.

Buy to Let Mortgages had only just been introduced and it was the heyday of 'carpet-baggers' as financial organisations de–mutualised. My 'young and adventurous' husband carpet bagged like a true professional and turned a modest investment into a significant sum of money, which he then reinvested into property.

Being young, retirement didn't even feature on his radar and he utilised the rise in house prices (following the Recession of the early 90's) to leverage his capital and increase his property portfolio.

These initial investments were in Bristol, where we lived at the time, and by the time our careers moved us along the M4 corridor, we had established a portfolio of six houses. It was 1999. Settling in Berkshire was considerably more expensive and so we made the decision to sell three properties to allow us to buy our new home. (Would we do it differently now? – most probably!)

The Buy–To–Let phenomenon was rapidly taking off and our careers were in full flow. As established landlords we foolishly considered ourselves 'seasoned investors' and let complacency creep in. We subsequently extended our portfolio by an additional three houses, taking us back to six houses, even though we exercised minimal due diligence.

Life then dealt what felt like an extremely harsh blow, as my husband was made redundant from his corporate role.

We now recognise this to be the catalyst that introduced him to the world of Mortgage Broking, however at the time it was a shock and difficult to accept. Two years later, however, a twist of fate gave us the opportunity to purchase one of the mortgage businesses my husband had been working for and Alton Mortgages Ltd came into existence.

The next few years were manic, business boomed, and our children were born. I went part–time, but continued to juggle a corporate career, and my husband's business rapidly exploded from the tiny study he had been allocated, encroaching onto our kitchen table and our lives. There was only one thing for it – we needed to move to a larger property. March 2007 we moved to our new home and took on a bigger mortgage.

My corporate career was enjoyable but with two young children and long hours it was very intense. Alton Mortgages was thriving so we made the decision that I would resign and join our family business. My move was 18 months in the planning and I studied my mortgage exams in the evenings and weekends. My goal was to be a qualified Mortgage Broker and self employed by the time our daughter started school. I hit my target and left behind my generous salary, company car, final salary pension and bonuses on the 31st August 2007.

At the time we had no idea of the shape of things to come, the country was booming and no–one foresaw the impact of the American issues on the world's financial situation. As always, hindsight is a wonderful thing and the following quote is taken from an article published in the Guardian on 1st December 2011.

'The former boss of Northern Rock, Adam Applegarth, pinpointed the start of the first credit crunch as 9 August 2007. It was the "day the world changed," he said.'

So in–fact, unbeknown to me at the time, I chose to leave the safety of my corporate position just 22 days after the Credit Crunch had started.

Over the next year the Credit Crunch bit hard. Our mortgage business struggled and revenue was severely down on the previous high.

We refocused our attentions on Life Cover and Insurances, believing our remaining income was 'safe' as we were diversified. But we failed to recognise there was a fundamental flaw in our judgement. All of our earned income for business completed with the Banks and Insurance firms was paid to our Mortgage network (for whom we were an Appointed Representatives under the FSA Guidelines), prior to it being paid to us. When our mortgage network went into Administration in 2009, owing its Brokers more than £2m, we lost another £25k of earnings, all of which we had struggled to achieve during the difficult times.

To add insult to injury we were then prevented from trading for two and a half weeks as we were required to follow the FSA's Guidelines and register with a new mortgage network. It seemed there was no way of hastening this transition.

We felt the pain financially!

However, they do say there are lessons to learn in life and dealing with adversity certainly teaches you a few. We learnt three fundamentally important lessons.

1. Parents are indeed wise when they teach you to keep some money back for the 'rainy days', because 'rainy days' do happen. Having been careful in the good years helped us tremendously.

2. If this was what retirement was going to be like – 'time on your hands, but acute money worries' – it wasn't the retirement we were dreaming of. We knew at that point we never wanted to be in that financial situation again.

3. We learnt first–hand the value of receiving regular rental income.

This experience combined with reading 'Rich Dad, Poor Dad' by Robert Kiyosaki was the catalysis which re–focused our attention on building an asset base that would provide for us financially. We wanted to ensure our retirement was as 'golden' as we had been promised with 'peace of mind' in the preceding years.

Together we decided property investment was going to be our route to financial security and we set about utilising equity within our home, to provide an investment pot. As I had free time it made sense I should take the lead on investing, however my first priority was to re–educate myself so that I could invest wisely.

We knew first–hand that cash–flow was our goal.

With this in mind I analysed locations close to home, before looking at Nottingham (my husband's home City). I went on the same journey I discuss in this book, assessing cash–flow potential against mitigating our risk on voids etc, and then finally considering capital growth.

Our initial investment pot could buy two houses in the South East, but eight in Nottingham. I had no doubt that capital growth in the South East of England would be quicker when the market changed but the combined capital growth from eight smaller properties further North would be almost the same. As Nottingham offered the advantage of greater yields, and our key investment criteria was cash flow, the decision was clear.

In February 2010 I started investing again for our family and since then I have added to our portfolio a total of 13 houses, taking our total to 19 (well 18.5 really, as we own one jointly with friends).

Alton Property Partners, my Hands–Free investment business was established in June 2010, as it became clear that the connections I had established were valuable to others looking to achieve the same financial security. Particularly those who were unable to dedicate the time to 'get it right', or for whom 'property investment' simply didn't light their fire. They welcomed the outcome, but didn't want to get physically involved and would rather pay for the expertise of another. To date I've had the privilege of purchasing and refurbishing a further 21 houses for investors.

Venus Property Mentoring followed shortly after as I wanted to share my investment knowledge, to help and encourage more women into the world of property investment. However, bizarrely my first Mentee was a male and the mix has remained approximately 50/50 even since, so I recently rebranded my mentorship business as Alton Property Mentoring. Uniquely, I designed all of my mentoring programmes to incorporate one to one time with my Mind Coach, as I know exactly how nerve–wracking it can be on your own, going out and taking those first investment steps. I wanted my Mentees to be prepared with technical knowledge, backed up with inner confidence and self–drive.

So has my property journey always been easy? No

Have there been learning curves along the way? Most definitely

Am I happy that we made the decision to take control of our futures? Absolutely!

None of us are getting any younger, but I have the peace of mind of knowing we have made provision for our golden years. And in addition we have paved the way for our children to have financial security in years to come.

Importantly, my journey also developed within me the burning passion to write this book, because I fear so many are unwittingly ill prepared for retirement, sleep–walking into a future of financial pain. They simply haven't realised they have the opportunity to make decisions now that could change the course of their lives.

Interestingly, a recent survey by book publishers, Haynes, to create the Top 20 Bucket List items found that when asked 'What would you most like to do with all that spare time when you retire? 21% of 55 year olds said 'Write a book'. The sixth most popular item.

I've simply brought my timeline forward … and rightfully so, as item No 15 on the list was 'Invest in Property'. However, by now I hope you will have realised that if you leave the investing until you reach retirement your horse will have bolted, and the opportunity will have been lost.

It's important to me that as you have read this book you have realised how I detest hype and 'get rich quick' schemes (probably as a result of being brought up by two very grounded parents – an Accountant and an Engineer). After–all there are enough such schemes already and we have all heard of horror stories where people have been conned out of large sums of money.

My drive in writing this book has been simple, my focus has been clear –to share the nuts and bolts of sound investment for cash–flow. I want people to make sensible, fact based decisions to meet their own personal circumstances and not be misled by superficially inflated figures.

I know it's not sexy but it works!!

I hope you have enjoyed reading this book as much as I have enjoyed the challenge of writing it, and your future is improved by the knowledge you now possess to influence the decisions you take.

Finally, if you would like to understand more about my business offerings please find these detailed in the following 4 pages.

Your Own
15 Step Retirement Rescue Plan

A Personal One–to–One service to plan your financial future

This is a one–to–one service designed specifically for anyone who having read this book has realised they have a Pension Shortfall and wants help to Rescue their Retirement via investing in property. The session will provide the opportunity to discuss your personal circumstances, so together we can create your own 15 Step Retirement Rescue Plan.

Together we will discuss the following:

- Your retirement income requirement
- Your current pension plans and performance
- Your current pension outlook and shortfall
- Your current financial circumstances and future mortgage capacity. This will involve spending time with an Independent Mortgage Broker (my husband) who can provide you with up to date financial advice.
- Your investment approach – which is the best fit for you.
- Your investment area in the UK.
- How to financially analyse a property for investment purposes.

You will be provided with copies of my own documentation to take away.

For more information please go to my website:
www.gillalton.com

Alton Property Partners

Alton Property Partners is established to provide an investment service for those who wish to invest in property to support their Pension Plan, but for whom life is already too busy. The service is very much designed to provide a personal service and as such client numbers are limited.

Alton Property Partners specialise in utilising the knowledge, skills and connections of a powerful team of experienced professionals to deliver investment properties 'stress free' to clients.

As all the hard–work is completed by the team, clients of Alton Property Partners can relax and have the peace of mind knowing that they are making sound financial decisions to support their Retirement, without having to take on additional workload.

Please refer to my website for further details.

Website address:
www.altonpropertypartners.co.uk

Alton Property Mentoring

Alton Property Mentoring (previously known as Venus Property Mentoring) offers one–to–one Property Mentoring designed specifically to support those who are looking to venture into property investment for the first time.

The comprehensive programmes work at the pace of the individual and ensure all Mentees understand the key fundamentals for investing success, so they can go forth and invest with confidence.

There are three programmes to choose from, Silver, Gold or Platinum so Mentees can select the programme which best suits their individual needs. Each programme includes time with both myself and my Mind Coach as the key to your success is based on the equation below.

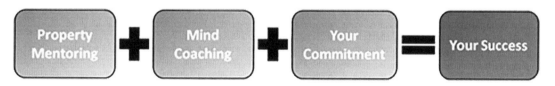

For more information on the programmes please refer to the website:
www.altonpropertymentoring.co.uk

Alton Mortgages Ltd

Alton Mortgage Ltd is a whole of market, Independent Mortgage Brokerage which has been trading since 2005.

Offering a wealth of knowledge on Residential and Buy To Let mortgages you can be assured of a highly professional and personal service.

Alton Mortgages Ltd is also able to support their clients with preferential Insurance quotations, as well as provide Life Cover and Critical Illness Cover.

For more information on how Alton Mortgages can help you, please call
Tel: 01628 560820. Or go to www.altonmortgages.co.uk

Glossary of Terms

a

Allowable Expenses

Those business costs that can be set against profit before the tax liability is calculated.

Annuity Rate

Normally quoted as a percentage which, when applied to your saved pension pot determines the annual income you will receive in retirement.

c

Cash–flow

The amount of money received after mortgage and all property costs have been paid. A consistently positive cash–flow puts money into your pocket month by month.

Compound Growth Rate

The 'growth rate' is the annual percentage by which an investment grows. 'Compound' confirms that interest earned is added to the original capital and reinvested, so will itself earn interest in future years.

CPI (Consumer Price Index)

A measure of inflation based on the cost of a fixed basket of products and services, including housing, electricity, food and transportation. The CPI is published monthly. It is also called the cost–of–living index.

Credit Crunch

A sudden sharp reduction in the availability of money or credit from banks and other lenders.

d

DD (Due Diligence)

The steps taken by an individual to gather important/ influential information to enable sound financial decisions to be made.

Defined Benefit Pension

The employer promises a specific monthly benefit in retirement which is pre–determined by a formula based on the employee's earnings history, service and age.

Defined Contribution Pension

A pension where the payout is reliant upon the amount of money contributed and the performance of the investment vehicle.

e

Early Redemption Charges

A charge made by the Mortgage Lender if the borrower terminates a mortgage in advance of the terms of that particular mortgage.

Escrow Account

An account held by a third party on behalf of two other parties in a transaction. The funds are held by the escrow service until it receives the appropriate written or oral instructions, or until obligations have been fulfilled.

f

FCA (Financial Conduct Authority)

The Financial Conduct Authority replaced the Financial Services Authority. It regulates financial firms that provide services to consumers and maintains the integrity of the UK's financial markets.

Freehold

The permanent legal ownership of property and/or land, providing all debts thereon have been cleared.

FSA (Financial Services Authority)

Replaced by the Financial Conduct Authority

Funding for Lending Scheme

An initiative introduced in July 2012 to incite banks to lend to UK households and businesses. The Bank of England lends to banks and building societies at very low rates of interest on the understanding that this money is passed on to borrowers and not used to improve Balance Sheets. This incentive has been instrumental in reducing mortgage interest rates, but is bad news for Savers.

g

Gearing (also known as Financial Leverage)

Long term debt compared to equity. Normally expressed as a percentage. For example, a 25% deposit on a property would mean the gearing is 75%.

GRY (Gross Rental Yield)
The annual rental income, expressed as a percentage of the purchase price of the property. This figure is a basic measure for comparing one property against another, but does not take into account the full property costs associated with investing.

Guerrilla Marketing
A marketing tactic in which a company uses surprise and / or unconventional methods to promote a product or service. From a property investment viewpoint it includes yellow boards on lampposts, signs at Traffic Lights and on parked vans etc.

h

Hands–Free Investing
The due diligence and the ground work are provided as a paid service to the investor, who is then able to benefit from a property portfolio with the minimum of personal effort.

Highly Geared
The same as Highly Leveraged. Where a large amount of money is borrowed in relation to the amount of capital (equity) held by the borrower.

i

IFA (Independent Financial Adviser)
A professional who offers advice on financial matters such as stocks and shares and, because they are not tied to one specific Bank, is able to recommend products from the whole of the market.

Independent Mortgage Broker
A Mortgage Broker who can source mortgage and insurance products from the whole of market, and is not tied to one specific Bank.

l

Leasehold
Allows the use of property for a given period of time e.g. 99, 60 or 30 years, after which it reverts to the landowner who then takes legal possession.

Leverage
Using borrowed capital for an investment with the aim of producing profits that exceed the interest payable on the loan.

LTV (Loan to Value)
The value of the loan expressed as a percentage of the value of the asset purchased.

n

Negative Equity
The outstanding loan on a property is greater than the value of that property

Net Rental Yield
The annual rental income, less costs, expressed as a percentage of the value of the property.

Normal Distribution Curve
A mathematical graph that shows how often a particular result will be produced.

o

Off Plan
Selecting a property on the basis of drawings and specifications and purchasing before the property is built.

Over–geared
Borrowings are too high in relation to the capital / equity within a property. This can put extreme pressure on finances and the ability to remortgage.

Over–gearing
Allowing the borrowings to rise too high in relation to the equity held within a property.

Over–leveraged
Same as Over–geared.

p

Pension Protection Fund
A statutory fund supported by levies charged on eligible defined benefit pension schemes. If an employer with an eligible scheme become insolvent and there are insufficient assets in company's pension scheme, members are compensated by the Pension Protection Fund.

Ponzi Scheme

A scheme which pays returns to its investors from their own money or from the money paid by subsequent investors, rather than from the profits earned by the individual or organization running the operation.

Portfolio Building Company

A company that contracts to build a specific portfolio of properties for an investor, for example 5 houses within 6 years. This is often promised on the basis of just one initial deposit.

q

Quantitative Easing

The Bank of England buys Government and corporate bonds from banks and other financial institutions to increase the money supply and promote lending.

r

RPI (Retail Price Index)

A measure of inflation. It includes slightly different elements from the CPI basket of goods and the formula is calculated differently. Many think this is a more accurate reflection of the 'true cost of living'. RPI normally runs about 0.9% higher than CPI.

Return on Investment (ROI)

A useful formula to quantify the performance efficiency of an investment. The net gain from the investment is divided by the cost of the investment and the result is expressed as a percentage.

s

SIPP

Self Invested Pension Scheme.

t

Total Expense Ratio

A measure of the total annual cost of a fund to the investor.

u

Unencumbered

A property that is free from any encumbrances, such as mortgages or debt secured on the property.

Figures within this Book

Sources of Information

Websites Utilised

- www.hl.co.uk/pensions/interactive–calculators/pension–calculator
- www.hl.co.uk/pensions/annuities/annuity–best–buy–rates
- www.hmrc.gov.uk
- www.nationwide.co.uk/hpi/datadownload/data_download.htm
- www.hmrc.gov.uk/cgt/property/calc–cgt.htm
- www.ons.gov.uk/ons/dcp171778_270487.pdf
- www.actuaries.org.uk/research–and–resources/documents/cmi–mortality–projections–model–cmi2012
- www.which.co.uk/money/insurance/guides/insurance–gender–discrimination–rules/gender–directive–overview/
- www.lv.com/adviser/working–with–lv/news_detail/?articleid=2860606
- www.gov.uk/government/statistical–data–sets/live–tables–on–rents–lettings–and–tenancies)
- www.architecture.com/NewsAndPress/News/RIBANews/News/2012/Timetoendtheblightofpoor UKhousinggroundbreakingnationalinquirycallsforUKhousingrevolution.aspx#.UdxtniRwYdU
- www.ons.gov.uk/ons/rel/vsob1/divorces–in–england–and–wales/2011/sty–what–percentage–of–marriages–end–in–divorce.html
- www.uplandsdaycentre.co.uk/2013/04/revitalising–day–centre/
- www.swanlowpark.co.uk/cpirpimonthly.jsp
- www.investmentweek.co.uk/investment–week/news/2164061/performing–shares–ftse–decade
- www.rentright.co.uk/rrpi
- lha–direct.voa.gov.uk/search.aspx
- www.payscale.com/research/UK/
- www.hmrc.gov.uk/cgt/intro/basics.htm#5
- www.taxcafe.co.uk/resources/capital_gains_tax_allowances.html
- homelet.co.uk/rentalindex/regional–map
- www.housepricecrash.co.uk/
- www.mortgagestrategy.co.uk/
- www.moneyvista.com/guides–tools/retirement–pensions/understanding–your–pension–statement/
- www.enterprisezones.communities.gov.uk/enterprise–zone–map/

- www.rightmove.co.uk
- www.nethouseprices.com
- www.zoopla.co.uk
- www.mouseprice.com
- www.police.UK
- www.enterprisezones.communities.gov.uk
- www.themovechannel.com/calculators

Source Data for Figures

- **Figure 3:**
  Office for National Statistics
- **Figure 4:**
  Office for National Statistics
- **Figure 5:**
  www.monevator.com/what–is–ter/
- **Figure 6:**
  www.actuaries.org.uk (Institute of Faculty of Actuaries)
- **Figure 7:**
  www.nationwide.co.uk/hpi/datadownload/data_download.htm
- **Figure 9:**
  www.hl.co.uk/pensions/annuities/annuity–best–buy–rates
- **Figure 15:**
  www.themovechannel.com/calculators
- **Figure 49:**
  www.hmrc.gov.uk
- **Figure 58:**
  www.payscale.com

Articles Reviewed

- http://www.moneywise.co.uk/news/2012–05–24/one–five–brits–has–no–pension
- http://www.publications.parliament.uk/pa/cm201314/cmselect/cmtreasy/writev/qe/qe.pdf
- http://www.telegraph.co.uk/comment/4077140/A–century–after–its–birth–is–the–state–pension–on–its–last–legs.html

- http://www.parliament.uk/documents/commons/lib/research/rp99/rp99–111.pdf
- http://www.telegraph.co.uk/earth/greenpolitics/population/9402836/Census–2011–How–the–population–has–changed–in–the–last–100–years.html
- http://www.dailymail.co.uk/news/article–2326105/Teachers–NHS–staff–pension–income–slashed–third.html
- http://www.bbc.co.uk/news/business–15925017 http://www.telegraph.co.uk/finance/personalfinance/pensions/9523765/Pensions–are–being–cut–by–the–Bank–of–England–Saga–report–warns.html
- http://blogs.spectator.co.uk/coffeehouse/2012/08/qe–the–ultimate–subsidy–for–the–rich/
- http://www.corecities.com/
- http://www.nottinghamcity.gov.uk/index.aspx?articleid=1381
- http://www.mailonsunday.co.uk/money/pensions/article–2192504/Bank–England–slammed–claim–QE–scheme–harmed–pensions.html
- http://www.dwp.gov.uk/newsroom/press–releases/2012/may–2012/dwp058–12.shtml
- http://www.thisismoney.co.uk/money/investing/article–2077187/2012–stock–market–predictions–What–shares.html
- http://en.wikipedia.org/wiki/Income_in_the_United_Kingdom
- http://www.actuarialpost.co.uk/article/uk———039worst–in–the–worldat–saving–for–retirement———039–4409.htm
- http://www.telegraph.co.uk/finance/personalfinance/pensions/9882001/Brits–worst–in–world–at–saving–for–retirement.html
- http://www.telegraph.co.uk/finance/personalfinance/pensions/9325041/UK–pension–performance–among–worst–in–developed–world.html
- http://www.telegraph.co.uk/finance/personalfinance/pensions/9915075/Baby–boomers–admit–their–biggest–financial–regret.html
- http://www.telegraph.co.uk/finance/personalfinance/savings/9873834/How–Britain–is–giving–up–on–saving.html
- http://www.telegraph.co.uk/finance/personalfinance/pensions/9888179/Pension–savers–fall–New–low–in–workers–saving–for–retirement.html
- http://www.guardian.co.uk/society/datablog/2012/jun/22/household–incomes–compare
- http://www.standardlife.co.uk/1/site/uk/financial–education/retirement–planning/retirement–income
- http://www.thisismoney.co.uk/money/mortgageshome/article–2313731/Interest–mortgage–timebomb–force–400–000–homes.html
- http://www.thisismoney.co.uk/money/mortgageshome/article–1671748/House–prices–What–expect—news–predictions.html

- http://www.telegraph.co.uk/finance/personalfinance/investing/9918427/Five–tips–for–buy–to–let–investors.html
- http://www.thisismoney.co.uk/money/news/article–1607881/When–UK–rates–rise.html
- http://www.telegraph.co.uk/finance/personalfinance/pensions/9918390/How–annuity–firms–clean–up–at–your–expense.html
- http://www.bbc.co.uk/news/business–11619379
- http://www.telegraph.co.uk/finance/personalfinance/pensions/9956321/Retired–women–earn–6500–less–than–men.html
- http://www.thisismoney.co.uk/money/pensions/article–2260256/Retiring–2013–3–400–worse–2008.html
- http://www.telegraph.co.uk/finance/personalfinance/pensions/9882001/Brits–worst–in–world–at–saving–for–retirement.html
- http://www.dailymail.co.uk/money/mortgageshome/article–2288742/Ticking–timebomb–endowment–shortfalls–leave–400–000–facing–home–sale.html
- http://www.guardian.co.uk/money/2013/feb/27/auto–enrolment–pensions–employees–opt–out
- http://www.telegraph.co.uk/finance/personalfinance/consumertips/household–bills/9892984/How–prices–changed–over–30–years.html
- http://www.economist.com/node/457272
- http://www.telegraph.co.uk/finance/personalfinance/pensions/9888179/Pension–savers–fall–New–low–in–workers–saving–for–retirement.html
- http://www.housepricecrash.co.uk/forum/index.php?showtopic=187477
- http://www.dailymail.co.uk/news/article–2275985/75–000–cap–cost–care–lost–thousands–pensioners–homes.html
- http://www.dailymail.co.uk/money/pensions/article–2262084/Nine–million–workers–counting–lottery–win–windfall–pay–retirement.html
- http://www.telegraph.co.uk/finance/personalfinance/pensions/9826640/Pensioners–face–a–lifetime–of–paying–off–debts.html
- http://www.thisismoney.co.uk/money/mortgageshome/article–2272349/It–getting–easier–obtain–mortgage–large–deposit–At—banks–offer–help–time–buyers.html
- http://www.newsrt.co.uk/news/fancy–an–income–of–41–000–in–retirement–then–you–ll–hit–the–new–pension–lifetime–limit–of–1–25m–1039684.html
- http://www.thisismoney.co.uk/money/pensions/article–2243037/David–Burnett–lost–fifth–pension—unfair–rules.html
- http://www.telegraph.co.uk/finance/budget/9725594/Autumn–Statement–2012–state–pension–rises–by–2.70–per–week.html

- http://www.ifaonline.co.uk/ifaonline/news/2229687/osborne–cuts–pension–tax–relief–to–gbp40k
- http://www.dailymail.co.uk/money/pensions/article–2243848/Autumn–Statement–Middle–classes–dragged–pension–tax–trap.html
- http://www.thisismoney.co.uk/money/news/article–2245025/Will–win–lose–George–Osbornes–tax–squeeze.html
- http://www.telegraph.co.uk/finance/personalfinance/pensions/9693320/Young–professionals–expect–a–pension–of–30000.html
- http://www.telegraph.co.uk/finance/personalfinance/pensions/9599885/Pensions–Poor–annuity–rates–risk–jeopardising–the–entire–auto–enrolment–project.html
- http://www.telegraph.co.uk/finance/personalfinance/pensions/9596584/Annuity–rates–fall–by–7pc–in–three–months.html
- http://www.telegraph.co.uk/finance/personalfinance/pensions/9687517/Badly–written–law–could–deprive–4m–of–their–pensions.html
- http://www.telegraph.co.uk/finance/newsbysector/retailandconsumer/9688214/Young–people–have–entirely–unrealistic–pension–assumptions.html
- http://www.thisismoney.co.uk/money/experts/article–2194772/My–wifes–pension–fund–worth–paid–Where–invest–money.html
- http://www.dailymail.co.uk/money/pensions/article–2233371/Four–landlords–live–rent–pension.htmlhttp://www.bbc.co.uk/news/uk–20176858 Pension projections cut by FSA to stop 'false impressions'
- http://www.bbc.co.uk/news/business–18117305
- http://www.thisismoney.co.uk/money/pensions/article–2203691/Should–stay–opt–enrolment–revolution–pensions.html
- http://www.thisismoney.co.uk/money/pensions/article–2202619/How–plug–pension–shortfall–Ideas–boosting–retirement–income.html
- http://www.thisismoney.co.uk/money/mortgageshome/article–2212155/Investors–warned–risky–rich–quick–property–schemes–U–S.html
- http://www.ft.com/cms/s/0/624a2340–0890–11e2–b37e–00144feabdc0.html#axzz28mG8qUTA
- http://www.propertyhawk.co.uk/index.php?page=magazine&id=214
- http://www.telegraph.co.uk/news/uknews/9462426/Almost–half–of–Brits–are–not–planning–to–use–a–pension–when–retire.html
- http://www.thisismoney.co.uk/money/pensions/article–2117755/If–youre–50–planning–retirement–beware–2027–pension–apocalypse.html
- http://www.bbc.co.uk/news/business–18883932
- http://www.bbc.co.uk/news/business–18923014http://www.express.co.uk/finance/personalfinance/338227/New–pensions–scheme–won–t–deliver–enough

- http://www.bbc.co.uk/news/business–19060716
- http://money.uk.msn.com/mortgages–and–homes/cliffside–house–demolished–in–landslide
- http://www.thisismoney.co.uk/money/pensions/article–2327474/Fifth–retiring–year–poverty–line.html
- http://www.telegraph.co.uk/finance/personalfinance/9849057/Average–household–water–bill–to–rise–by–3.5pc–to–388–a–year.html
- http://www.ofgem.gov.uk/Markets/RetMkts/rmr/smr/Pages/indicators.aspx
- http://www.telegraph.co.uk/finance/personalfinance/consumertips/household–bills/9680091/British–families–need–25000–just–to–survive.html
- http://money.aol.co.uk/2013/03/06/10–000–cost–of–basic–pensioner–living/
- http://www.motester.co.uk/mot–general–information/mot–information–for–motorists/mot–price–list–and–information
- http://www.theaa.com/motoring_advice/running_costs/
- http://www.dentalcentres.co.uk/dentist–fees–nhs.php
- http://www.jrf.org.uk/sites/files/jrf/minimum–income–standards–2012–full.pdf
- http://www.thisismoney.co.uk/money/bills/article–2042014/How–does–cost–dog–cat.html
- http://www.theguardian.com/money/2011/oct/07/pet–insurance–worth–it
- http://www.tvlicensing.co.uk/about/media–centre/news/how–much–does–a–tv–licence–cost–FAQ23/

5270550R00148

Printed in Great Britain
by Amazon.co.uk, Ltd.,
Marston Gate.